PHARMACOVIGILANCE
CONCEPTS AND APPLICATIONS FOR DRUG SAFETY

MURALIDHAR RAO AKKALADEVI

Contents

PREFACE

Pharmacovigilance is an essential aspect of ensuring the safety and efficacy of medications. It involves detecting, assessing, understanding, and preventing adverse effects or any other drug-related problems. The field of pharmacovigilance is constantly evolving with the development of new methods, regulations, and guidelines aimed at improving the safety of medications.

"Pharmacovigilance: Concepts and Applications for Drug Safety" is a comprehensive guide to the field of pharmacovigilance, covering all aspects of drug safety monitoring and reporting. The book provides an in-depth overview of the principles and practices of pharmacovigilance, including its history, regulatory framework, and methods for evaluating medication safety data.

In recent years, there has been a growing interest in pharmacovigilance, as more and more people become aware of the potential risks associated with medications. This has led to an increase in the number of pharmacovigilance programs around the world, as well as the development of new methods for detecting and assessing adverse drug reactions.

Additionally, the emergence of new technologies such as artificial intelligence and machine learning has created new opportunities for pharmacovigilance, allowing for more efficient and accurate detection of adverse drug reactions. As the field of pharmacovigilance continues to evolve, it will play an increasingly important role in ensuring the safety and efficacy of medications for patients worldwide.

Dr.Muralidhar Rao Akkaladevi
04-01-2023
Hyderabad

PHARMACOVIGILANCE

Concepts and applications for Drug safety
Dr.Muralidhar Rao Akkaladevi
Dean of Studies
St.Mary's college of Pharmacy
Secunderabad

Published by Notion press
Notion Press, Inc.
800, West EI Camino Real #180,
California USA 94040
Notion Press Media Pvt Ltd,
#7, Red Cross Road,
Egmore, Chennai, Tamil Nadu 600008
Email ID: publish@notionpress.com
Phone Number: +91 44 46315631

Syllabus (PCI)

UNIT - I
Introduction to Pharmacovigilance:

- History and development of Pharmacovigilance
- Importance of safety monitoring of Medicine
- WHO international drug monitoring programme
- Pharmacovigilance Program of India (PvPI)

Introduction to adverse drug reactions:

- Definitions and classification of ADRs
- Detection and reporting
- Methods in Causality assessment
- Severity and seriousness assessment
- Predictability and preventability assessment

Basic terminologies used in pharmacovigilance:

- Terminologies of adverse medication related events
- Regulatory terminologies

UNIT – II
Drug and disease classification:

- Anatomical, therapeutic and chemical classification of drugs
- International classification of diseases
- Daily defined doses

Drug dictionaries and coding in pharmacovigilance:

- WHO adverse reaction terminologies
- MedDRA and Standardized MedDRA queries

- WHO drug dictionary

  Information resources in pharmacovigilance:

- Basic drug information resources

  Establishing pharmacovigilance programme:

- Establishing in a hospital
- Establishment & operation of drug safety department in industry
- Contract Research Organizations (CROs)

UNIT – III
Vaccine safety surveillance:

- Vaccine Pharmacovigilance
- Vaccination failure
- Adverse events following immunization

Pharmacovigilance methods:

- Passive surveillance – Spontaneous reports and case series
- Stimulated reporting
- Active surveillance – Sentinel sites, drug event monitoring and registries
- Comparative observational studies – Cross sectional study, case control study and cohort
- study
- Targeted clinical investigations

UNIT – IV
Safety data generation:

- Pre-clinical phase

- Clinical phase
- Post approval phase

ICH Guidelines for Pharmacovigilance

- Organization and objectives of ICH
- Expedited reporting
- Individual case safety reports
- Periodic safety update reports
- Post approval expedited reporting
- Pharmacovigilance planning
- Good clinical practice in pharmacovigilance studies

UNIT – V

Pharmacogenomics of adverse drug reactions

- Genetics related ADR with example focusing PK parameters

Drug safety evaluation in special population

- Pediatrics
- Pregnancy and lactation
- Geriatrics

CIOMS

- CIOMS Working Groups
- CIOMS Form

CDSCO (India) and Pharmacovigilance

- D&C Act and Schedule Y
- Differences in Indian and global pharmacovigilance requirements

I

Introduction to Pharmacovigilance

Pharmacovigilance is a branch of pharmacology that deals with the safety and effectiveness of medicines. The term pharmacovigilance comes from the Greek words "pharmakon" meaning drug and "vigilare" meaning to keep watch. The primary objective of pharmacovigilance is to detect, assess, understand, and prevent adverse effects or any other drug-related problems that might occur during or after the use of a medicinal product.

Pharmacovigilance is an important aspect of public health that aims to ensure the safe and effective use of medicines. The use of medicinal products is widespread, and it is imperative that their safety is monitored continuously to detect and prevent any adverse effects. The ultimate goal of pharmacovigilance is to ensure that patients are protected from harm and receive maximum benefit from the use of medicines.

Pharmacovigilance is a relatively new field that has gained significant importance over the years. It has evolved as a science over time, and its development can be traced back to the thalidomide disaster of the 1960s. Thalidomide was a medication that was widely used to treat nausea and vomiting during pregnancy. However, it was later found to cause severe birth defects in newborns. This event was a turning point in the history of pharmacovigilance, and it led to the establishment of the World Health Organization's (WHO) International Drug Monitoring Programme in 1968.

The primary objective of pharmacovigilance is to detect adverse effects and other drug-related problems that may occur during or after the use of a medicinal product. Adverse effects are defined as any unwanted or harmful reaction to a medicine that occurs at doses used for prophylaxis, diagnosis, or treatment. It is essential to understand and identify adverse effects, as they can range from mild to severe and may even be life-threatening in some cases.

Pharmacovigilance involves the collection, analysis, and interpretation of data related to adverse effects and other drug-related problems. This information is then used to inform healthcare professionals and the public about the risks associated with the use of medicines. Pharmacovigilance is not limited to the identification of adverse effects. It also involves understanding the factors that contribute to the occurrence of these effects, such as patient characteristics, medication errors, and drug interactions.

The importance of pharmacovigilance cannot be overstated. The use of medicines is an integral part of healthcare, and adverse effects can have a significant impact on patients' quality of life. The timely detection and prevention of adverse effects are crucial in ensuring patient safety and preventing harm. Therefore, pharmacovigilance plays a vital role in public health and the safe use of medicines.

1.1.1 History and development of Pharmacovigilance

Pharmacovigilance, the science of monitoring and evaluating the safety and effectiveness of medicines, has a rich history that dates back to the early 1960s. It was in this decade that the thalidomide disaster occurred, which caused the birth of thousands of deformed babies due to the use of the drug during pregnancy. This tragedy led to the establishment of the first national pharmacovigilance system in the UK in 1964, which was followed by other countries such as France, Canada, and the United States.

The importance of pharmacovigilance continued to grow as more drugs were developed and marketed. In the 1970s, the World Health Organization (WHO) established the International Drug Monitoring Program to collect and analyze adverse drug reaction (ADR) reports from member countries. The program was later expanded and became the WHO Programme for International Drug Monitoring, which continues to operate today as a global pharmacovigilance network.

In the 1990s, the development of new drugs and the globalization of the pharmaceutical industry led to an increased need for pharmacovigilance. This resulted in the establishment of the International Conference on Harmonization (ICH) in 1990, which aimed to develop standardized guidelines for the development, registration, and post-approval monitoring of medicines. ICH guidelines are now widely recognized and followed by regulatory authorities and pharmaceutical companies worldwide.

The 21st century saw further developments in pharmacovigilance, with the emergence of new technologies and the increasing use of data analytics in drug safety monitoring. The digital age has enabled the automation of ADR reporting and the development of new methods for signal detection and analysis.

Pharmacovigilance has become an integral part of the drug development process, with the ultimate goal of ensuring the safety and efficacy of medicines for patients. It has evolved from a reactive system to a proactive one, with the aim of preventing adverse events before they occur. The importance of pharmacovigilance cannot be overstated, as it plays a crucial role in safeguarding public health and improving patient outcomes.

1.1.2 Basic principles of Pharmacovigilance

Pharmacovigilance is a crucial aspect of healthcare that deals with the detection, assessment, understanding, and prevention of adverse effects or any other drug-related problems. It involves continuous monitoring of the safety and efficacy of medicines in real-world settings, ensuring that the benefits of using a drug outweigh its risks. The basic principles of Pharmacovigilance are essential for ensuring the safety and quality of drugs and promoting public health.These are as follows

1. To collect and analyze data on drug safety

This includes data on adverse drug reactions (ADRs) from healthcare providers, patients, and other sources such as regulatory agencies and clinical trials. The data is then analyzed to determine the frequency, severity, and causality of ADRs, as well as any other drug-related problems such as drug interactions, misuse, or abuse.

2. To communicate drug safety information to healthcare professionals, patients, and the public

This involves providing accurate and timely information on the risks and benefits of using a drug, including any new safety concerns that may arise. Communication can take many forms, including alerts, warnings, labeling changes, or educational campaigns.

3. To evaluate the effectiveness of risk minimization measures

Risk minimization measures are actions taken to reduce the risk of harm from a drug, such as dose adjustments, patient monitoring, or restrictions on use. Evaluating the effectiveness of these measures involves assessing whether they are achieving their intended goals and whether they are causing any unintended consequences.

4. To promote collaboration and cooperation among stakeholders

This includes healthcare professionals, regulatory agencies, pharmaceutical companies, patients, and other interested parties. Collaboration and cooperation are essential for sharing information, identifying safety concerns, and developing and implementing risk minimization strategies.

5. To promote transparency and accountability

This involves providing clear and accurate information on drug safety, including any limitations or uncertainties in the data. It also involves taking responsibility for any errors or omissions in drug safety information and taking appropriate actions to address them.

6. To promote continuous improvement

This involves continuously evaluating and improving drug safety monitoring systems, risk minimization measures, and communication strategies. It also involves conducting research to address gaps in knowledge and identify new safety concerns.

1.1.3 Regulatory agencies involved in Pharmacovigilance

Regulatory agencies play a critical role in Pharmacovigilance by overseeing the safety and efficacy of medicines throughout their lifecycle. These agencies set the standards for drug approval and monitoring, enforce compliance with regulations, and take action to mitigate risks and promote public health. Here are some of the key regulatory agencies involved in Pharmacovigilance:

US Food and Drug Administration (FDA): The FDA is responsible for regulating the safety and efficacy of drugs in the United States. It reviews new drug applications and conducts post-marketing surveillance to monitor the safety and effectiveness of approved drugs. The FDA also issues safety alerts and warning letters to companies when safety concerns arise.

European Medicines Agency (EMA): The EMA is responsible for regulating the safety and efficacy of drugs in the European Union. It reviews drug applications and conducts post-marketing surveillance to monitor the safety and effectiveness of approved drugs. The EMA also issues safety alerts and recommendations to healthcare professionals and the public.

Pharmaceuticals and Medical Devices Agency (PMDA): The PMDA is the regulatory agency responsible for overseeing the safety and efficacy of drugs and medical devices in Japan. It reviews drug applications and conducts post-marketing surveillance to monitor the safety and effectiveness of approved drugs. The PMDA also issues safety alerts and recommendations to healthcare professionals and the public.

Health Canada: Health Canada is responsible for regulating the safety and efficacy of drugs and medical devices in Canada. It reviews drug applications and conducts post-marketing surveillance to monitor the safety and effectiveness of approved drugs. Health Canada also issues safety alerts and recommendations to healthcare professionals and the public.

World Health Organization (WHO): The WHO is responsible for promoting public health globally. It provides guidance and support to countries in the area of Pharmacovigilance and drug safety monitoring. The WHO also collaborates with other regulatory agencies to promote global drug safety standards and guidelines.

In addition to these agencies, many other national and international regulatory agencies are involved in Pharmacovigilance. These agencies work together to ensure that drugs are safe and effective for patients, and that healthcare providers have access to accurate and up-to-date information on drug safety. By collaborating and sharing information, regulatory agencies can promote public health and prevent harm from drugs.

1.1.4 *The role of healthcare professionals and patients in Pharmacovigilance*

Healthcare professionals and patients play a crucial role in Pharmacovigilance by reporting adverse drug reactions (ADRs) and other drug-related problems to regulatory agencies. Reporting ADRs is a voluntary process, and healthcare professionals and patients are encouraged to report any suspected ADRs, even if they are uncertain about the causality of the reaction. Here are some of the key roles of healthcare professionals and patients in Pharmacovigilance:

Healthcare professionals: Healthcare professionals, including doctors, pharmacists, nurses, and other healthcare providers, are often the first to identify and report ADRs. They have a responsibility to monitor patients for potential ADRs and report any suspected reactions to regulatory agencies. Healthcare professionals can also contribute to Pharmacovigilance by providing accurate and complete information on drug safety to their patients and colleagues.

Patients: Patients can play a vital role in Pharmacovigilance by reporting any suspected ADRs or other drug-related problems to their healthcare providers or regulatory agencies. Patients can also contribute to Pharmacovigilance by providing accurate and complete information on their medical history, medication use, and any allergies or sensitivities to drugs.

Pharmacists: Pharmacists have an important role in ensuring the safe use of drugs. They can contribute to Pharmacovigilance by identifying and reporting ADRs, providing information on drug safety to patients and healthcare professionals, and monitoring drug interactions and other drug-related problems.

Regulatory agencies: Regulatory agencies rely on reports of ADRs and other drug-related problems to monitor the safety and effectiveness of drugs. Healthcare professionals and patients are a crucial source of information for regulatory agencies, and their reports can help to identify new safety concerns and inform regulatory decisions.

Pharmaceutical companies: Pharmaceutical companies are also responsible for monitoring the safety and efficacy of their products. They can contribute to Pharmacovigilance by collecting and analyzing safety data, conducting post-marketing surveillance, and reporting ADRs to regulatory agencies.

1.1.5. Importance of Pharmacovigilance in Public Health

Pharmacovigilance plays a critical role in ensuring the safety of medications and protecting public health. Here are some examples of the importance of pharmacovigilance in public health:

Early detection of adverse drug reactions (ADRs): Pharmacovigilance allows for the early detection of ADRs, which can help prevent serious harm to patients. For example, in 2010, a safety alert was issued for the diabetes medication rosiglitazone due to concerns about an increased risk of heart attacks. This alert was based on data from pharmacovigilance systems that identified a possible safety signal.

Identification of previously unknown risks: Pharmacovigilance can help identify previously unknown risks associated with medications. For example, in the early 2000s, concerns were raised about the risk of suicidal behavior in children and adolescents taking certain antidepressant medications. This concern was based on data from pharmacovigilance systems that identified a possible safety signal.

Improving medication safety: Pharmacovigilance can help improve medication safety by identifying safety concerns and implementing measures to address them. For example, in 2007, the US Food and Drug Administration (FDA) implemented a risk evaluation and mitigation strategy (REMS) for the medication isotretinoin, which is used to treat severe acne. The REMS was designed to address safety concerns related to the risk of birth defects and psychiatric adverse events.

Enhancing patient safety: Pharmacovigilance helps enhance patient safety by ensuring that healthcare professionals and patients have access to up-to-date information about the risks and benefits of medications. For example, the FDA requires that medications have a package insert that includes information about ADRs, drug interactions, and other safety information.

II

Importance of safety monitoring of medicine

Safety monitoring, also known as drug safety monitoring or pharmacovigilance, refers to the process of identifying, evaluating, understanding, and preventing adverse drug reactions (ADRs) or other drug-related problems. It involves monitoring the safety and effectiveness of drugs throughout their lifecycle, from preclinical development and clinical trials to post-marketing surveillance and ongoing monitoring.

The goal of safety monitoring is to ensure that drugs are safe and effective for patients and to minimize the risks associated with their use. This is achieved through the collection and analysis of safety data, including reports of ADRs, clinical trial data, and other sources of information. Safety monitoring also involves the development and implementation of risk management plans, the dissemination of safety information to healthcare professionals and patients, and the collaboration with regulatory agencies to ensure the safe use of drugs.

The importance of safety monitoring cannot be overstated, as it is essential for identifying and managing safety risks associated with drug use. Safety monitoring helps to ensure that drugs are only approved and marketed if their benefits outweigh their risks, and that any safety concerns are identified and addressed promptly. It also helps to promote public health by ensuring the safe and effective use of drugs and by providing healthcare professionals and patients with up-to-date information on drug safety.

2.1 Why is Safety Monitoring important?

Safety monitoring is critical to ensuring the safety and effectiveness of drugs for patients. Here are some of the key reasons why safety monitoring is important:

Identification of safety concerns: Safety monitoring helps to identify safety concerns associated with drug use, including adverse drug reactions (ADRs) and other drug-related problems. This is essential for ensuring that patients are not exposed to unnecessary risks and that any safety concerns are addressed promptly.

Assessment of risk-benefit ratio: Safety monitoring allows for the assessment of the risk-benefit ratio of drugs. This helps to ensure that drugs are only approved and marketed if their benefits outweigh their risks, and that any safety concerns are managed appropriately.

Post-marketing surveillance: Safety monitoring continues after drugs are approved and marketed, allowing for the detection of safety concerns that may not have been identified during clinical trials. This is essential for ensuring that drugs are safe and effective in real-world settings.

Development of risk management plans: Safety monitoring helps to develop risk management plans to minimize the risks associated with drug use. This includes the implementation of measures to prevent or mitigate ADRs, such as monitoring for drug interactions and providing clear prescribing information to healthcare professionals.

Dissemination of safety information: Safety monitoring ensures that safety information is disseminated to healthcare professionals and patients, allowing them to make informed decisions about drug use. This includes the provision of up-to-date information on the safety of drugs, as well as any changes to prescribing information or risk management plans.

2.2 Types of Safety Monitoring

There are several types of safety monitoring that are important in pharmacovigilance. These include:

Spontaneous reporting: Spontaneous reporting involves the collection of reports of adverse drug reactions (ADRs) from healthcare professionals and patients. These reports are submitted voluntarily and can provide important information on the safety of drugs. For example, the spontaneous reporting of ADRs led to the discovery of serious liver toxicity associated with the use of the drug troglitazone, which ultimately led to its withdrawal from the market.

Clinical trials: Clinical trials are used to assess the safety and effectiveness of drugs before they are approved and marketed. Safety monitoring during clinical trials involves the collection and analysis of safety data, including ADRs and other drug-related problems. For example, during the clinical trials for the weight loss drug fen-phen, it was discovered that the drug was associated with serious heart valve problems, which ultimately led to its withdrawal from the market.

Post-marketing surveillance: Post-marketing surveillance involves the monitoring of the safety and effectiveness of drugs after they have been approved and marketed. This can involve the collection and analysis of safety data from a variety of sources, including spontaneous reports, observational studies, and clinical trials. For example, post-marketing surveillance of the drug rofecoxib (Vioxx) led to the discovery of an increased risk of heart attacks and strokes, which ultimately led to its withdrawal from the market.

Risk management plans: Risk management plans are developed to minimize the risks associated with the use of drugs. This can involve the implementation of measures to prevent or mitigate ADRs, such as monitoring for drug interactions, providing clear prescribing information to healthcare professionals, and educating patients about the safe use of drugs. For example, the risk management plan for the acne medication isotretinoin includes a pregnancy prevention program to minimize the risk of birth defects associated with the drug.

Case study: Thalidomide Thalidomide was a drug that was marketed in the 1950s and 1960s as a treatment for morning sickness in pregnant women. It was later discovered that the drug was responsible for causing severe birth defects, including limb deformities. The tragedy of thalidomide led to the development of the modern system of drug regulation and safety monitoring , and highlighted the importance of rigorous safety monitoring in drug development and approval. Thalidomide was approved for use without adequate testing for safety in pregnant women, and the tragedy that followed resulted in the development of stricter regulations for drug approval and safety monitoring.

The thalidomide tragedy also led to the establishment of the World Health Organization's Programme for International Drug Monitoring, which oversees the collection and analysis of spontaneous reports of ADRs from around the world. The programme has been instrumental in the detection of safety concerns associated with drugs, including the discovery of a rare but serious skin reaction associated with the use of the anticonvulsant drug carbamazepine.

2.3 Benefits of Safety Monitoring:

The benefits of safety monitoring in pharmacovigilance are numerous and significant. Safety monitoring can help to detect and manage adverse drug reactions (ADRs), ensure the safety and effectiveness of drugs, and ultimately improve patient outcomes. Some of the key benefits of safety monitoring include:

Early detection of ADRs: Safety monitoring can help to detect ADRs early, before they become widespread and cause serious harm to patients. For example, safety monitoring of the anti-inflammatory drug rofecoxib (Vioxx) led to the detection of an increased risk of heart attacks and strokes, which ultimately led to the drug's withdrawal from the market.

Improved patient safety: Safety monitoring can help to improve patient safety by identifying and managing potential safety concerns associated with drug use. For example, the implementation of a pregnancy prevention program as part of the risk management plan for the acne medication isotretinoin has helped to reduce the risk of birth defects associated with the drug.

Improved drug efficacy: Safety monitoring can also help to improve drug efficacy by identifying and managing factors that can affect a drug's effectiveness. For example, safety monitoring of the use of the anticoagulant drug warfarin has helped to identify factors that can affect the drug's effectiveness, such as genetic variations that affect the metabolism of the drug.

Improved public health: Safety monitoring can contribute to the improvement of public health by identifying and managing safety concerns associated with drugs, ultimately leading to better health outcomes for patients. For example, the discovery of serious liver toxicity associated with the use of the anti-diabetes drug troglitazone led to the drug's withdrawal from the market, preventing further harm to patients.

Case study: Thalidomide The thalidomide tragedy serves as a powerful reminder of the importance of safety monitoring in pharmacovigilance. The use of thalidomide by pregnant women led to severe birth defects, and the tragedy that followed led to the development of modern drug regulations and safety monitoring practices. Since then, safety monitoring has played a critical role in detecting and managing safety concerns associated with drugs, ultimately leading to improved patient outcomes.

2.4 Limitations of Safety monitoring

While safety monitoring is a critical component of pharmacovigilance, it is important to recognize that there are limitations to the process. Some of the key limitations of safety monitoring include:

Underreporting: One of the most significant limitations of safety monitoring is underreporting. Not all ADRs are reported to regulatory authorities, and some may go undetected altogether. For example, a study conducted in the United States found that only 1-10% of ADRs are actually reported to the FDA.

Bias: Bias can also be a limitation of safety monitoring. For example, certain types of ADRs may be more likely to be reported than others, leading to a skewed understanding of the risks associated with a particular drug.

Confounding factors: Confounding factors, such as co-morbidities or concomitant drug use, can also complicate the process of safety monitoring. For example, a patient may experience an ADR that is actually caused by a different drug they are taking, rather than the drug being monitored.

Limited sample size: Safety monitoring may be limited by the size of the patient population being monitored. This can be particularly relevant for rare ADRs, which may be difficult to detect in a small patient population.

Timing: Safety monitoring may be limited by the timing of the monitoring process. For example, some ADRs may not become apparent until months or years after a drug has been approved and has entered widespread use.

Case study: Avandia The case of the diabetes drug Avandia serves as an example of some of the limitations of safety monitoring. Avandia was approved for use in 1999, but concerns about the drug's safety began to emerge in the early 2000s. Studies suggested that the drug increased the risk of heart attack and stroke, but it wasn't until 2010 that the FDA limited the use of the drug due to safety concerns.

The Avandia case highlights the limitations of safety monitoring, particularly the potential for underreporting and the timing of safety concerns. It also underscores the need for ongoing safety monitoring of drugs throughout their lifecycle, even after they have been approved for use.

2.5 Challenges in implementing Safety Monitoring

While safety monitoring is an essential component of pharmacovigilance, there are several challenges that can make implementing safety monitoring difficult. Some of the key challenges include:

Lack of resources: One of the most significant challenges in implementing safety monitoring is a lack of resources. Monitoring ADRs requires significant investment in terms of time, staff, and funding. In some cases, particularly in low- and middle-income countries, resources may be limited, making it challenging to implement effective safety monitoring programs.

Data management: Safety monitoring requires effective data management systems to ensure that ADR reports are collected, analyzed, and acted upon in a timely manner. However, managing large volumes of data can be challenging, particularly when data is coming from multiple sources.

Communication: Effective communication is essential for safety monitoring to be successful. This includes communication between regulatory agencies, healthcare professionals, and patients. However, communication can be challenging, particularly in situations where language barriers or cultural differences exist.

Adverse event attribution: Determining whether an ADR is actually caused by a particular drug can be challenging. ADRs can be caused by a range of factors, including other medications, underlying health conditions, and patient behavior.

Case study: Thalidomide The thalidomide tragedy serves as an example of some of the challenges in implementing safety monitoring. Thalidomide was a medication that was prescribed to pregnant women in the 1950s and early 1960s to alleviate morning sickness. However, it was later discovered that thalidomide caused severe birth defects in thousands of children. The thalidomide tragedy highlights the challenges of ensuring medication safety, particularly in the context of limited data and inadequate safety monitoring practices.

III

World Health Organization International Drug monitoring Programme

3.1 Overview of the WHO international drug monitoring programme

The WHO international drug monitoring programme, also known as the WHO Programme for International Drug Monitoring, was established in 1968 to promote pharmacovigilance on a global scale. The programme operates in collaboration with national pharmacovigilance centres around the world, as well as with the Uppsala Monitoring Centre (UMC) in Sweden, which serves as the coordinating centre for the programme.

The main objectives of the programme are to detect and evaluate adverse drug reactions (ADRs), facilitate the rational use of medications, and promote public health and safety. This is achieved through the collection, analysis, and dissemination of information on the safety of medications. The programme also aims to increase awareness of the importance of pharmacovigilance among healthcare professionals, regulators, and the public.

National pharmacovigilance centres collect reports of suspected ADRs from healthcare professionals, patients, and other sources, and submit them to the UMC for analysis. The UMC then adds the data to a global database called VigiBase, which currently contains over 23 million individual case safety reports. The UMC also provides support and training to national centres, as well as conducting research on pharmacovigilance topics.

The WHO Collaborating Centre for International Drug Monitoring, located at the UMC, also plays an important role in the programme. The collaborating centre provides technical assistance to countries without a national pharmacovigilance centre, as well as conducting research and training activities.

The WHO international drug monitoring programme has had a significant impact on medication safety worldwide. It has contributed to the identification of previously unknown ADRs, as well as the removal of medications from the market due to safety concerns. The programme has also helped to raise awareness of pharmacovigilance and the importance of medication safety among healthcare professionals and the public.

However, the programme also faces several challenges, including the need for increased resources and funding, as well as the need for more effective communication and collaboration among stakeholders. Additionally, the evolving nature of pharmacovigilance challenges, such as the rise of herbal and alternative medicines, presents ongoing challenges for the programme.

Despite these challenges, the WHO international drug monitoring programme remains an important component of global efforts to ensure medication safety and promote public health.

3.2: *History of the WHO international drug monitoring programme*

Early initiatives in pharmacovigilance can be traced back to the mid-20th century, when reports of serious adverse reactions to medications began to emerge. These reports led to increased concern about medication safety and the need for systematic monitoring of medication use.

In the 1950s and 1960s, several countries, including the UK and the US, established pharmacovigilance programmes to monitor medication safety. However, it became clear that a coordinated global effort was needed to address the increasing globalization of the pharmaceutical industry and the widespread use of medications around the world.

In response to this need, the WHO Programme for International Drug Monitoring was established in 1968. The programme was created with the goal of facilitating global cooperation in pharmacovigilance, and to ensure that adverse drug reactions were identified and evaluated in a consistent and standardized manner.

Initially, the programme consisted of just 10 member countries, but it has since grown to include over 150 countries. The Uppsala Monitoring Centre (UMC) in Sweden was designated as the coordinating centre for the programme, and has played a critical role in its evolution.

Over time, the programme has evolved to adapt to new challenges and changes in the pharmaceutical industry. For example, the programme has expanded its focus to include monitoring of herbal and traditional medicines, as well as vaccines and other biologics.

The programme has also increased its emphasis on data analysis and signal detection, using advanced data mining techniques to identify potential safety concerns. In addition, the programme has increased its efforts to engage healthcare professionals and the public in pharmacovigilance activities, recognizing the importance of their participation in ensuring medication safety.

3.3 *Objectives of the WHO international drug monitoring programme*

To detect and evaluate ADRs: The primary objective of the programme is to detect and evaluate adverse drug reactions (ADRs) associated with the use of medications. This is achieved through the collection of spontaneous reports of suspected ADRs from healthcare professionals and the public. The programme aims to identify new and emerging safety concerns related to medications, and to evaluate the risks and benefits of medications in order to inform decisions about their use.

For example, the WHO international drug monitoring programme played a key role in identifying the link between thalidomide and birth defects in the 1960s. Spontaneous reports of birth defects in infants born to mothers who had taken thalidomide during pregnancy led to the withdrawal of the drug from the market in many countries. This highlighted the importance of systematic monitoring of medication safety, and led to the establishment of the WHO international drug monitoring programme.

To facilitate the rational use of medications: Another objective of the programme is to promote the rational use of medications. This involves ensuring that medications are used in the most appropriate and effective way, with a focus on minimizing harm and maximizing benefit. The programme aims to provide information to healthcare professionals and the public about the risks and benefits of medications, and to promote the use of evidence-based prescribing practices.

For example, the WHO international drug monitoring programme has played a role in promoting the rational use of antibiotics, through its efforts to monitor and address the emergence of antibiotic resistance. The programme has also provided guidance on the use of medications during pregnancy and breastfeeding, to help ensure that medications are used safely and appropriately.

To promote public health and safety: The overall objective of the programme is to promote public health and safety, by improving the safety and effectiveness of medications. This involves identifying and addressing safety concerns related to medications, and promoting the use of safe and effective medications.

For example, the WHO international drug monitoring programme has played a role in ensuring the safety of vaccines. The programme monitors the safety of vaccines through the collection of spontaneous reports of suspected ADRs, as well as through active surveillance and monitoring of vaccine safety during clinical trials. This has helped to ensure that vaccines are safe and effective, and has contributed to the control of vaccine-preventable diseases.

3.4 Operation of the WHO international drug monitoring programme

Data Collection and Analysis

The WHO international drug monitoring programme collects data from different sources, including healthcare professionals, patients, and regulatory agencies, to identify and evaluate adverse drug reactions (ADRs). This data is essential for promoting patient safety and improving the rational use of medications.

It is crucial that reporting of ADRs is accurate and complete to enable proper identification and analysis of safety concerns. The WHO encourages healthcare professionals and patients to report any suspected ADRs promptly. National pharmacovigilance centers (NPCs) play a crucial role in collecting and analyzing ADR reports from healthcare professionals, patients, and regulatory agencies.

To ensure consistent and standardized data collection and analysis, the WHO international drug monitoring programme utilizes coding systems such as MedDRA (Medical Dictionary for Regulatory Activities). The use of standardized terminology and coding systems ensures consistency in data collection and analysis.

Data analysis techniques such as signal detection and data mining are used to identify potential safety concerns. Signal detection involves identifying unusual patterns or trends in the data, while data mining involves analyzing large amounts of data to identify potential safety signals. Examples of successful data analysis leading to drug withdrawals or label changes include the case of rofecoxib/Vioxx, a COX-2 inhibitor that was withdrawn from the market due to an increased risk of cardiovascular events.

The WHO international drug monitoring programme also collaborates with other regulatory agencies to share data and identify potential safety concerns. The program works closely with the Uppsala Monitoring Centre, which is responsible for the scientific analysis of ADR reports and maintaining the WHO pharmacovigilance database.

National Pharmacovigilance Centers

National pharmacovigilance centers play a crucial role in the collection, analysis, and dissemination of information on adverse drug reactions (ADRs) at a country level. These centers serve as the primary source of ADR reports, which are then sent to the WHO international program for further analysis and evaluation. The establishment of these centers is a fundamental step in strengthening pharmacovigilance systems and improving patient safety.

The role of national pharmacovigilance centers includes the following:

Data collection: National centers receive ADR reports from healthcare professionals, patients, and regulatory agencies within their country. These reports are then compiled and entered into a national database.

Data analysis: National centers analyze the data collected to identify any potential safety concerns or emerging trends in the use of medicines. This analysis can also help to identify any population-specific risks associated with the use of medicines.

Dissemination of information: National centers play a critical role in disseminating information on ADRs to healthcare professionals and the general public. This information can help to increase awareness of potential risks associated with the use of medicines and improve patient safety.

However, national pharmacovigilance centers often face significant challenges. One major challenge is the lack of resources and expertise, particularly in low- and middle-income countries. This can make it difficult to collect and analyze ADR data effectively. Additionally, there may be cultural or language barriers that make it difficult for patients and healthcare professionals to report ADRs.

Despite these challenges, there have been successful national pharmacovigilance programs. For example, the Netherlands Pharmacovigilance Centre Lareb has established a strong network of healthcare professionals and patients to report ADRs. The center has also implemented innovative strategies, such as a mobile app, to make it easier for patients to report ADRs.

The Uppsala Monitoring Centre (UMC)

The Uppsala Monitoring Centre (UMC) is a key component of the WHO International Drug Monitoring Programme. It is an independent, non-profit organization located in Uppsala, Sweden, which coordinates the activities of the national pharmacovigilance centers in over 130 countries. The UMC was established in 1978 and since then, it has played a pivotal role in improving patient safety worldwide.

One of the major functions of the UMC is data analysis and signal detection. The UMC receives ADR reports from national pharmacovigilance centers around the world and stores them in VigiBase, its global database system. The UMC analyzes these reports using various statistical and data mining techniques to identify potential safety signals. These signals are further evaluated by the UMC and the national centers to determine whether regulatory action is necessary.

The UMC also plays a vital role in providing training and support for national centers. It conducts training programs and workshops for pharmacovigilance professionals, and provides technical assistance and advice on data analysis, signal detection, and other pharmacovigilance-related activities.

Another important contribution of the UMC is the development of the WHO Drug Dictionary, a standard reference tool for identifying and coding medicinal products. This dictionary provides a consistent terminology for use in pharmacovigilance activities and facilitates the sharing and comparison of data between different countries and regions.

The UMC has led several successful initiatives over the years. One example is the Vaccines Signal Investigation project, which was initiated by the UMC in response to concerns about the safety of pandemic influenza vaccines. The project involved the analysis of ADR reports from around the world to detect potential safety signals related to these vaccines. The project identified several potential safety issues, which were further investigated and addressed by regulatory authorities.

The WHO Collaborating Centre for International Drug Monitoring

The WHO Collaborating Centre for International Drug Monitoring was established in 2005 to support the WHO Programme for International Drug Monitoring. The center is based at the Uppsala Monitoring Centre in Sweden and serves as a hub for promoting pharmacovigilance worldwide.

The main role of the Collaborating Centre is to provide technical assistance and support to national pharmacovigilance centers in low- and middle-income countries. This includes training in ADR data collection, analysis, and reporting, as well as providing support for the development of national pharmacovigilance systems.

The Collaborating Centre also plays an important role in promoting international collaboration and sharing of pharmacovigilance information. It serves as a platform for discussion and knowledge exchange among national centers, regulatory authorities, and other stakeholders in the field of pharmacovigilance.

In addition, the Collaborating Centre is responsible for the development and dissemination of pharmacovigilance guidance and tools. This includes the development of the WHO Global Patient Safety Challenge on Medication Safety, which aims to improve the safety of medication use worldwide through the promotion of medication safety practices and the development of tools for reporting and preventing ADRs.

IV
Pharmacovigilance Program of India

4.1:Brief overview of the Pharmacovigilance Program of India (PvPI)

The Pharmacovigilance Program of India (PvPI) is a national program established by the Indian government to promote and monitor the safety of medicines used in the country. It was launched in July 2010 by the Ministry of Health and Family Welfare, in collaboration with the Indian Pharmacopoeia Commission (IPC) and the World Health Organization (WHO).

The PvPI has the primary objective of enhancing patient safety by promoting the reporting, detection, and analysis of adverse drug reactions (ADRs) in India. It is based on the principles of the WHO International Drug Monitoring Program and operates through a network of Adverse Drug Reaction Monitoring Centers (AMCs) across the country.

The PvPI has been instrumental in improving the safety of medicines in India by establishing a robust reporting system for ADRs. It has also helped in generating valuable information on the safety profile of medicines, which has been used to develop guidelines for their safe use.

Under the PvPI, healthcare professionals, including doctors, nurses, pharmacists, and other healthcare providers, are encouraged to report suspected ADRs to the AMCs. The reports are then analyzed by the IPC and the National Coordination Center (NCC), and appropriate actions are taken to ensure patient safety.

The PvPI also conducts various activities to create awareness about ADRs and pharmacovigilance among healthcare professionals and the general public. These activities include training programs, workshops, and conferences, among others.

One of the major achievements of the PvPI has been the development of a national database of ADRs, which is accessible to healthcare professionals and researchers. The database provides valuable information on the safety of medicines used in India and has been used to develop guidelines for their safe use.

4.2 History and Development of PvPI

India is one of the largest and fastest-growing pharmaceutical markets in the world, with a population of over 1.3 billion and a rapidly expanding healthcare industry. With the increased use of medications, the need for a comprehensive pharmacovigilance program became increasingly important.

The National Pharmacovigilance Centre (NPC) was established in 2005, under the Ministry of Health and Family Welfare, to monitor adverse drug reactions (ADRs) in India. However, it was realized that NPC alone cannot handle the growing burden of ADR monitoring, and there was a need for a more comprehensive pharmacovigilance program.

In 2010, the Ministry of Health and Family Welfare, Government of India, launched the Pharmacovigilance Program of India (PvPI) with the help of the World Health Organization (WHO). The program aimed to monitor, detect, assess, and prevent ADRs associated with medicines, medical devices, and vaccines in India.

PvPI was established to strengthen the NPC's activities and create a nationwide pharmacovigilance system, as well as to promote the rational use of medicines and improve patient safety. The program is implemented through a network of ADR monitoring centers (AMCs) across India, which are responsible for collecting and reporting ADRs. The program also provides training and support for healthcare professionals, patients, and pharmaceutical companies to encourage reporting of ADRs.

4.3 Objectives and goals of PvPI

The objectives of PvPI are aligned with the broader goal of promoting public health and safety by ensuring that medicines available in India are safe and effective. One of the key objectives is to monitor the safety of medicines in India, which involves collecting and analyzing data on adverse drug reactions (ADRs) associated with the use of medications. By identifying potential safety issues and taking appropriate actions, PvPI aims to minimize the risks associated with the use of medicines and improve patient outcomes.

In addition to monitoring the safety of medicines, PvPI also aims to create awareness about ADRs among healthcare professionals and the general public. This is crucial as lack of awareness about ADRs can lead to under-reporting, which in turn can hinder the detection and management of potential safety issues. Through various training programs and awareness campaigns, PvPI seeks to educate healthcare professionals and the general public about the importance of reporting ADRs and the role of pharmacovigilance in ensuring patient safety.

Another important objective of PvPI is to improve patient safety and public health through effective pharmacovigilance. This involves not only identifying potential safety issues but also taking appropriate actions to mitigate the risks associated with the use of medicines. For example, PvPI may recommend changes to product labels, issue safety alerts, or even recommend the withdrawal of a drug from the market if it poses an unacceptable risk to patients.

The objectives of PvPI are aligned with the broader goal of promoting public health and safety through effective pharmacovigilance. By monitoring the safety of medicines, creating awareness about ADRs, and taking appropriate actions to mitigate risks, PvPI aims to ensure that medicines available in India are safe and effective, and that patients receive the best possible care.

4.4 Structure and Operation of PvPI

Pharmacovigilance Program of India (PvPI) was established in 2010 with the objective of monitoring and improving drug safety in India. The program is coordinated by the National Coordination Centre (NCC) and operates through a network of Adverse Drug Reaction Monitoring Centers (AMCs) located in various parts of the country. PvPI's structure and operation are critical in promoting the reporting and monitoring of Adverse Drug Reactions (ADRs) and taking necessary regulatory actions to ensure patient safety.

The National Coordination Centre (NCC) is the central coordinating body of PvPI, responsible for collecting and analyzing data on ADRs. The NCC receives ADR reports from various sources, including healthcare professionals, patients, pharmaceutical companies, and regulatory authorities. The data collected by NCC is analyzed using data analysis techniques such as signal detection and data mining to identify potential safety issues.

The Adverse Drug Reaction Monitoring Centers (AMCs) are responsible for receiving, collating, and forwarding ADR reports to the NCC. There are currently 275 AMCs in India, and their functioning is critical in increasing ADR reporting. AMCs receive ADR reports from healthcare professionals, patients, and pharmaceutical companies, and ensure that the reports are of good quality, complete, and consistent.

PvPI has also established a Pharmacovigilance Advisory Committee (PAC), comprising experts from various fields, including medicine, pharmacology, toxicology, and regulatory affairs. The role of PAC is to review ADR reports and provide recommendations on drug safety issues to regulatory authorities. PAC recommendations have led to several regulatory actions in India, including the suspension and revocation of marketing authorization for certain drugs.

The role of healthcare professionals, patients, and pharmaceutical companies in reporting ADRs is crucial in ensuring drug safety. PvPI has implemented several initiatives to increase awareness about ADR reporting among healthcare professionals and patients. These initiatives include conducting training programs, workshops, and awareness campaigns to promote ADR reporting. Pharmaceutical companies are also encouraged to report ADRs to PvPI through their own pharmacovigilance systems.

One example of the impact of PvPI's structure and operation is the identification of previously unknown or underreported ADRs. For instance, in 2019, the NCC received several ADR reports related to the use of ranitidine, a commonly used drug for acid reflux. The reports indicated a potential risk of cancer associated with the long-term use of ranitidine. Following the reports, the regulatory authorities in India suspended the marketing authorization of ranitidine, and the drug was subsequently withdrawn from the market globally.

Another example of PvPI's impact is the revision of drug labels based on safety concerns. In 2018, the NCC received several reports of ADRs associated with the use of flupentixol and melitracen, a combination drug used to treat depression. The reports indicated a potential risk of cardiac arrhythmias and sudden cardiac death associated with the use of the drug. Following the reports, the regulatory authorities in India revised the drug label to include a warning about the potential cardiac risks.

The program's coordination through the NCC and the network of AMCs has enabled the timely collection, analysis, and dissemination of ADR reports. The involvement of healthcare professionals, patients, and pharmaceutical companies in reporting ADRs is also essential in identifying potential safety issues. The examples of the identification of previously unknown ADRs and the revision of drug labels illustrate the impact of PvPI's structure and operation in ensuring patient safety.

4.5 Collaboration and partnership with other national and international pharmacovigilance programs

The WHO provides technical support and guidance to countries in the establishment and strengthening of their pharmacovigilance systems. The WHO has also designated the Uppsala Monitoring Centre (UMC) as its collaborating center for international drug monitoring. PvPI has been collaborating with UMC for capacity building, training, and signal detection. Through this partnership, PvPI has received technical support for data analysis and signal detection, and also contributed to the UMC's global database of adverse drug reactions (ADRs), VigiBase. Additionally, PvPI is a member of the International Society of Pharmacovigilance (ISoP), which is a global non-profit organization that promotes pharmacovigilance worldwide. PvPI also collaborates with other national and international organizations such as the Indian Pharmacopoeia Commission (IPC), Central Drugs Standard Control Organization (CDSCO), and Indian Council of Medical Research (ICMR) to promote drug safety and pharmacovigilance in India. These collaborations have helped PvPI to leverage global expertise, enhance its capacity to monitor drug safety, and contribute to the development of international pharmacovigilance guidelines and standards.

4.5 Regulatory Action and Label Changes

The impact of PvPI on drug safety in India can also be seen in the regulatory actions taken by the Indian regulatory authorities, such as the Central Drugs Standard Control Organization (CDSCO), based on data from PvPI. The CDSCO is the national regulatory body for pharmaceuticals and medical devices in India, and is responsible for ensuring that drugs and medical devices available in the Indian market are safe and effective. Since its establishment, PvPI has been working closely with the CDSCO to improve drug safety in India.

One notable example of regulatory action taken based on data from PvPI is the suspension of the marketing authorization for the drug pioglitazone in India in 2013. Pioglitazone is a drug used to treat type 2 diabetes, but has been associated with an increased risk of bladder cancer. Data from PvPI showed an increased number of cases of bladder cancer in patients taking pioglitazone, leading the CDSCO to suspend the drug's marketing authorization in India. This action was taken to ensure patient safety and to prevent further harm from the use of pioglitazone.

Another example of the impact of PvPI on drug safety in India is the label changes made for certain drugs based on safety concerns identified through PvPI. For example, in 2016, the CDSCO recommended label changes for the drug tramadol, a pain medication, to warn of the risk of serotonin syndrome when used with other drugs that affect serotonin levels in the brain. This recommendation was made based on data from PvPI that showed an increased number of cases of serotonin syndrome associated with the use of tramadol in combination with other drugs affecting serotonin levels. This label change ensures that patients and healthcare professionals are aware of the potential risks associated with using tramadol in combination with other drugs, and can take appropriate precautions to prevent harm.

The impact of these regulatory actions and label changes on patient safety and public health in India cannot be overstated. They have helped to identify previously unknown safety issues with drugs and have ensured that appropriate action is taken to prevent harm. This has helped to build trust in the Indian healthcare system and has improved patient outcomes.

4.6 Impact of PvPI on Public Health and Safety

The establishment of the Pharmacovigilance Program of India (PvPI) has had a significant impact on patient safety and public health in India. The program has led to increased reporting and monitoring of adverse drug reactions (ADRs), regulatory action and label changes for drugs, and improved awareness and education among healthcare professionals and the general public.

One of the main impacts of PvPI has been the improved reporting and monitoring of ADRs. The program has encouraged healthcare professionals, patients, and pharmaceutical companies to report ADRs, resulting in an increase in the number of ADR reports. This has helped to identify previously unknown or underreported ADRs and has enabled the authorities to take appropriate action to ensure patient safety. The use of data analysis techniques, such as signal detection and data mining, has also helped to identify potential safety issues and take appropriate action.

The impact of these actions on patient safety and public health in India has been significant. By identifying and addressing safety concerns, PvPI has helped to reduce the risk of harm from medications and improve patient outcomes. The program has also helped to build trust in the healthcare system by ensuring that patients have access to safe and effective medications.

4.7 Awareness and Education

The role of pharmacovigilance programs such as PvPI in raising awareness about ADRs is crucial in improving patient safety and public health. Healthcare professionals play a vital role in detecting and reporting ADRs, and the awareness of ADRs among healthcare professionals is essential to improve the safety and efficacy of medications. PvPI has undertaken various educational initiatives and training programs to improve pharmacovigilance knowledge and practices among healthcare professionals and the general public.

PvPI has developed various educational materials, including posters, pamphlets, and brochures, to raise awareness about ADRs among the general public. These educational materials provide information about the importance of reporting ADRs, how to recognize and report ADRs, and the role of PvPI in ensuring drug safety. PvPI has also conducted various awareness programs and campaigns, such as the "Pharmacovigilance Awareness Week," to increase awareness about ADRs among the general public.

In addition to awareness programs for the general public, PvPI has also developed various training programs for healthcare professionals to improve their pharmacovigilance knowledge and practices. PvPI has collaborated with the Indian Pharmacopoeia Commission (IPC) to develop a national pharmacovigilance training program for healthcare professionals. The training program aims to provide comprehensive training on pharmacovigilance principles, ADR reporting, and data analysis techniques to improve the detection and reporting of ADRs. The training program is available in both online and offline formats to reach a larger audience.

Moreover, PvPI has also conducted various workshops, conferences, and seminars for healthcare professionals to discuss the latest developments in pharmacovigilance and share best practices. These events provide a platform for healthcare professionals to learn from each other's experiences and improve their pharmacovigilance knowledge and practices.

The impact of these awareness and education initiatives has been significant in improving patient safety and reducing the risk of harm from medications. The increased awareness of ADRs among healthcare professionals has led to more reporting of ADRs, which has resulted in the identification of previously unknown or underreported ADRs. The improved pharmacovigilance knowledge and practices among healthcare professionals have also led to more effective use of data analysis techniques, such as signal detection and data mining, to identify potential safety issues and take appropriate action.

4..8 The partnership between PvPI and the Indian Pharmacopoeia Commission (IPC) to develop a national pharmacovigilance training program for healthcare professionals

In order to achieve the goal of improving patient safety and public health through effective pharmacovigilance, PvPI has collaborated with various organizations to develop educational initiatives and training programs for healthcare professionals. One such collaboration is with the Indian Pharmacopoeia Commission (IPC) to develop a national pharmacovigilance training program.

The IPC is a scientific organization that sets standards for drugs and pharmaceuticals in India. It is responsible for establishing and updating the Indian Pharmacopoeia (IP), which is an official book of standards for drugs included in the Indian Pharmacopoeia. The IP is a legal document under the Drugs and Cosmetics Act and is intended to ensure the quality, safety, and efficacy of drugs marketed in India.

The partnership between PvPI and IPC aims to improve pharmacovigilance practices among healthcare professionals in India by developing a comprehensive training program. The program includes various aspects of pharmacovigilance, such as the importance of reporting ADRs, the process of reporting ADRs, and the analysis of ADR data to identify safety concerns.

The training program is designed to be accessible to healthcare professionals in all settings, including hospitals, clinics, and pharmacies. It is available in both online and offline formats to cater to the needs of a diverse group of healthcare professionals. The program is also available in multiple languages to ensure that it is accessible to healthcare professionals across India.

The impact of this collaboration can be seen in the increased awareness and reporting of ADRs by healthcare professionals in India. The training program has helped to improve the knowledge and skills of healthcare professionals in pharmacovigilance practices, which has resulted in better identification and reporting of ADRs. This, in turn, has helped to improve patient safety and public health by identifying and addressing safety concerns with drugs used in India.

In conclusion, the partnership between PvPI and IPC to develop a national pharmacovigilance training program for healthcare professionals is an important step towards improving pharmacovigilance practices in India. The training program has helped to raise awareness about ADR reporting, improve knowledge and skills of healthcare professionals, and ultimately improve patient safety and public health.

4.9 Examples and case studies:

The 2008 Ranbaxy Case: An Overview of Safety and Quality Concerns

The 2008 Ranbaxy case is a significant event in the history of pharmaceuticals in India, and it has had far-reaching implications for drug safety and regulation in the country. Ranbaxy Laboratories, one of the largest pharmaceutical companies in India, was accused by the US Food and Drug Administration (FDA) of violating good manufacturing practices, falsifying data, and failing to ensure the safety and quality of its products. The FDA banned the import of more than 30 Ranbaxy drugs, including popular medications such as the cholesterol-lowering drug Lipitor and the AIDS drug Viread.

The case was a wake-up call for the Indian pharmaceutical industry, which had until then been largely self-regulated. It highlighted the need for more rigorous oversight of drug manufacturing and distribution, and it led to a series of regulatory reforms and initiatives aimed at improving drug safety and quality in India.

One of the key developments that emerged from the Ranbaxy case was the establishment of the National Pharmacovigilance

Centre (NPC) in India in 2005. The NPC was set up to collect and analyze information on adverse drug reactions (ADRs) in India and to provide recommendations for drug safety. The center was later expanded and restructured into the Pharmacovigilance Program of India (PvPI) in 2010, which became a comprehensive national pharmacovigilance program.

PvPI has played a significant role in improving drug safety and regulation in India since its establishment. It has encouraged healthcare professionals, patients, and pharmaceutical companies to report ADRs, leading to increased reporting of previously unknown or underreported ADRs. Data analysis techniques, such as signal detection and data mining, have been used to identify potential safety issues and take appropriate action. This has resulted in regulatory actions and label changes for drugs based on safety concerns identified through PvPI.

PvPI has also played a crucial role in raising awareness about ADRs among healthcare professionals and the general public. Educational initiatives and training programs have been developed to improve pharmacovigilance knowledge and practices among healthcare professionals. These initiatives have had a positive impact on improving patient safety and reducing the risk of harm from medications.

The 2013 regulatory action against Johnson & Johnson in India

In 2013, the Indian government took regulatory action against Johnson & Johnson (J&J), one of the world's largest healthcare companies, over safety concerns related to its hip implants. The incident highlighted the importance of robust pharmacovigilance systems and regulatory oversight to ensure the safety of medical products in India.

The controversy began in 2010 when J&J recalled two types of hip implants – ASR XL Acetabular System and ASR Hip Resurfacing System – globally due to high failure rates. However, J&J continued to sell the devices in India for another two years, despite being aware of safety concerns. In 2013, the Indian regulatory authorities took action against J&J, banning the sale and distribution of the implants in India and ordering the company to pay compensation to affected patients.

The incident raised several important issues related to drug safety and regulatory oversight in India.

1.It highlighted the need for stronger regulatory measures to ensure that medical products are safe and effective before they are approved for sale in India. In this case, J&J was able to continue selling its hip implants in India despite safety concerns and regulatory action taken in other countries. This incident underscored the importance of harmonizing global regulatory standards and ensuring that companies follow the same safety protocols in all countries where they operate.

2.The incident highlighted the importance of robust pharmacovigilance systems to detect and respond to safety concerns related to medical products. The Johnson & Johnson case was a clear example of how pharmacovigilance data can be used to identify safety concerns related to medical products and trigger regulatory action. In this case, the adverse event reports submitted to PvPI were instrumental in raising concerns about the safety of J&J's hip implants and triggering regulatory action by the Indian authorities.

3. The incident emphasized the importance of patient safety and the need for compensation programs to support patients who are harmed by medical products. Following the regulatory action against J&J, the company established a compensation program for affected patients in India. This program was a step towards addressing the harm caused by the company's products, and it underscored the importance of ensuring that patients who are harmed by medical products receive appropriate support and compensation.

4.10 Challenges and Future Directions for PvPI

Pharmacovigilance Program of India (PvPI) has made significant progress in improving drug safety in India, but it still faces various challenges that need to be addressed to achieve its full potential. This essay will discuss the challenges faced by PvPI and future directions to overcome these challenges.

One of the main challenges faced by PvPI is the lack of resources and expertise. PvPI needs trained personnel to collect, analyze, and disseminate data on adverse drug reactions (ADRs). However, there is a shortage of qualified healthcare professionals with pharmacovigilance expertise in India. Additionally, many healthcare professionals are not aware of the importance of ADR reporting or lack the necessary training to identify and report ADRs. This lack of resources and expertise can limit the effectiveness of PvPI in identifying and managing ADRs.

To overcome this challenge, PvPI has initiated various capacity-building programs and training sessions for healthcare professionals to increase their knowledge of pharmacovigilance. For instance, PvPI has launched the "Pharmacovigilance Awareness Week" every year since 2015 to create awareness among healthcare professionals, patients, and the general public about the importance of ADR reporting. PvPI has also collaborated with the Indian Medical Association (IMA) to provide pharmacovigilance training to doctors and other healthcare professionals.

Another challenge faced by PvPI is the underreporting of ADRs. Despite the increase in ADR reporting since the establishment of PvPI, it is still believed that many ADRs go unreported. This is partly due to the lack of awareness and incentives for healthcare professionals to report ADRs. Additionally, patients may not report ADRs due to a lack of knowledge about ADRs or fear of legal consequences.

To address this challenge, PvPI has launched various initiatives to increase ADR reporting by healthcare professionals and patients. PvPI has collaborated with patient organizations to raise awareness among patients about the importance of ADR reporting. PvPI has also launched an online ADR reporting system that is user-friendly and accessible to healthcare professionals and patients.

Another challenge faced by PvPI is the limited reach of ADR monitoring in rural areas. Most of the ADR monitoring centers (AMCs) are located in urban areas, which makes it difficult to collect data on ADRs in rural areas. This can lead to underreporting of ADRs in these areas, which can have serious implications for patient safety.

To address this challenge, PvPI has launched various initiatives to increase the reach of ADR monitoring in rural areas. PvPI has collaborated with the National Rural Health Mission (NRHM) to establish AMCs in rural areas. PvPI has also launched a mobile application for ADR reporting, which can be accessed by healthcare professionals and patients in remote areas.

V

Introduction to Adverse Drug Reactions

5.1 Definitions of ADRs

An adverse drug reaction (ADR) is an unwanted or harmful reaction that occurs after the administration of a drug. It is an important consideration in pharmacotherapy because it can affect patient outcomes and overall drug safety. Definitions of ADR vary slightly across different organizations and regulatory bodies, but the general concept remains the same.

The World Health Organization (WHO) defines an ADR as "a response to a drug which is noxious and unintended, and which occurs at doses normally used in man for the prophylaxis, diagnosis, or therapy of disease, or for the modification of physiological function." This definition emphasizes that the response is unwanted and occurs at normal doses of the drug, rather than as a result of overdose or misuse.

The US Food and Drug Administration (FDA) defines an ADR as "any unexpected, unintended, undesired, or excessive response to a drug that occurs at usual doses." This definition adds the criteria of unexpectedness and excessiveness to the WHO definition.

The European Medicines Agency (EMA) defines an ADR as "a response to a medicinal product which is noxious and unintended, and which occurs at doses normally used in man for the prophylaxis, diagnosis or therapy of disease or for the modification of physiological function." This definition is similar to the WHO definition, but adds the term "medicinal product" to include both drugs and other forms of therapy.

Regardless of the specific definition used, the underlying concept of an ADR is that it is a harmful or unwanted response that occurs as a result of drug use. ADRs can range from mild, such as nausea or dizziness, to severe, such as anaphylaxis or liver failure, and can occur with any drug.

The identification and reporting of ADRs is critical for patient safety and the continued monitoring of drug safety. Healthcare professionals, patients, and pharmaceutical companies all play important roles in identifying and reporting ADRs. Understanding the definitions of ADR and their various interpretations across different organizations and regulatory bodies is an important aspect of pharmacovigilance and ensuring drug safety.

5.2 Classification of ADRs

ADRs can occur due to various factors such as drug-drug interactions, drug-disease interactions, genetic factors, and environmental factors. These reactions can manifest immediately after drug administration or can occur after a prolonged duration of drug usage. ADRs can be classified based on various parameters such as the type of reaction, severity, and mechanism of action.

The classification of ADRs is important for several reasons.

1. First, it helps healthcare professionals and regulatory agencies to understand the nature and frequency of ADRs associated with a particular drug or class of drugs. This information is critical in making decisions about drug safety and in developing strategies

for managing ADRs.

2. Second, the classification of ADRs helps in identifying new or emerging safety concerns related to specific drugs or classes of drugs.

3. Third, it helps in standardizing the terminology used to describe ADRs, which is important for effective communication between healthcare professionals and regulatory agencies.

5.2.1 Classification based on the type of reaction

ADRs can be classified into six major categories: Type A, Type B, Type C, Type D, Type E, and Type F.

1. Type A reactions, also known as Augmented reactions, are predictable and dose-dependent. These reactions occur due to the pharmacological action of a drug and are typically related to its therapeutic effect. For example, gastrointestinal bleeding caused by nonsteroidal anti-inflammatory drugs (NSAIDs) or drowsiness caused by antihistamines.

2. Type B reactions, also known as Bizarre reactions, are unpredictable and not dose-dependent. These reactions occur due to the idiosyncratic nature of an individual and are not related to the pharmacological action of a drug. For example, severe allergic reactions to penicillin or aspirin-induced asthma.

3. Type C reactions, also known as Continuous reactions, are chronic and dose-dependent. These reactions occur due to prolonged exposure to a drug and are typically related to its pharmacological effect. For example, osteoporosis caused by long-term use of corticosteroids or tardive dyskinesia caused by long-term use of antipsychotics.

4. Type D reactions, also known as Delayed reactions, occur after a prolonged period of drug exposure and are typically related to a drug's effect on the body's immune system. For example, drug-induced lupus caused by certain medications.

5. Type E reactions, also known as End-of-treatment reactions, occur after the cessation of drug therapy and are typically

related to the rebound effect of the drug. For example, rebound hypertension caused by abrupt discontinuation of certain antihypertensive medications.

6. Type F reactions, also known as Failure of therapy reactions, occur when a drug fails to produce the desired therapeutic effect. For example, treatment failure in cancer patients due to drug resistance.

In addition to the above classification, ADRs can also be classified based on the severity of the reaction. The severity can range from mild, such as a rash or nausea, to severe, such as death or permanent disability. The severity of an ADR is determined by the extent of the harm caused to the patient and the level of medical intervention required to manage the reaction. A mild ADR may not require any treatment or intervention, while a severe ADR may require hospitalization, intensive medical care, and long-term treatment. Severe ADRs can also lead to permanent disability or death. Classifying ADRs based on severity is important for prioritizing patient care, determining the appropriate course of action, and identifying potential safety issues with drugs. ADR severity can also impact the regulatory decision-making process, such as the decision to withdraw a drug from the market or revise its label. Therefore, it is crucial to accurately assess and classify the severity of ADRs to ensure patient safety and improve pharmacovigilance practices.

5.2.2 Classification of ADRs developed by WHO

can be done in several ways based on various criteria such as severity, time of occurrence, dose, mechanism, and organ system affected. One common classification system is the one developed by the World Health Organization (WHO) called the Adverse Reaction Terminology (ART). ART is a hierarchical classification system that uses a coded format to describe ADRs based on the body system affected, the severity of the reaction, and the drug involved.

The first level of ART classification divides ADRs into system organ classes (SOCs) based on the affected body system, such as gastrointestinal disorders, skin disorders, and nervous system disorders. The second level of classification divides SOCs into high-level group terms, which describe more specific aspects of the reaction such as the nature, duration, or outcome of the reaction. For example, the high-level group term "hypersensitivity and allergic reactions" describes ADRs such as anaphylactic shock, urticaria, and angioedema.

The third level of classification in ART is the preferred term (PT), which describes the specific ADR. PTs are coded using a five-digit alphanumeric code, where the first two digits represent the SOC, the third digit represents the high-level group term, and the last two digits represent the PT. For example, the PT code for anaphylactic shock is "100001."

5.2.3 Classification of ADRs developed by Council for International Organizations of Medical Sciences (CIOMS)

The CIOMS classification system uses a five-point grading scale to classify ADRs based on their severity. The grading system ranges from mild to fatal, with grades 1-2 indicating mild to moderate reactions, and grades 3-5 indicating severe to fatal reactions.

In addition to these classification systems, ADRs can also be classified based on the time of occurrence, dose, mechanism, and organ system affected. For example, ADRs can be classified as immediate or delayed based on the time of onset, and as dose-related or non-dose-related based on the relationship to the dose of the drug. ADRs can also be classified based on the mechanism of action, such as immunologic, non-immunologic, or idiosyncratic.

Proper classification of ADRs is essential for effective pharmacovigilance, as it helps in identifying the most serious and common ADRs associated with different drugs. This information can be used to develop appropriate risk mitigation strategies, such as label changes, drug withdrawals, and patient monitoring. It also helps in improving drug safety by identifying previously unknown or underreported ADRs.

Classification of ADRs is an important aspect of pharmacovigilance, as it helps in understanding the nature, severity, and frequency of ADRs associated with different drugs. Various classification systems are available based on different criteria such as severity, time of occurrence, dose, mechanism, and organ system affected. Accurate and consistent classification of ADRs is essential for effective pharmacovigilance and improving drug safety.

VI
Detection and Reporting of Adverse Drug Reactions

6.1 Introduction:

Adverse Drug Reactions (ADRs) are defined as any harmful or unwanted effects that occur as a result of exposure to a medication. ADRs can range from mild reactions such as a rash or nausea to severe reactions such as organ failure or death. Detection and reporting of ADRs is an essential aspect of pharmacovigilance, which is the science and activities related to the detection, assessment, understanding, and prevention of adverse effects or any other drug-related problem.

6.2 Importance of ADR Detection and Reporting:

The detection and reporting of ADRs are crucial for ensuring patient safety and drug effectiveness. The potential consequences of undetected or underreported ADRs can be severe, leading to patient harm, disability, and even death. For example, in 2004, Merck & Co. voluntarily withdrew the pain reliever Vioxx from the market due to an increased risk of heart attacks and strokes, which was not detected in clinical trials. It is estimated that Vioxx caused between 88,000 to 139,000 heart attacks in the US alone.

In addition to patient safety, ADR detection and reporting can also have significant financial implications. Drug recalls and lawsuits resulting from ADRs can cost pharmaceutical companies billions of dollars. Furthermore, undetected ADRs can lead to increased healthcare costs due to the need for additional medical interventions.

Role of Pharmacovigilance:

Pharmacovigilance is a vital aspect of drug safety that involves the monitoring, detection, and prevention of ADRs. It plays a significant role in ensuring that drugs are safe and effective, and that any risks associated with their use are identified and minimized.

Pharmacovigilance activities include the collection, analysis, and dissemination of information on the safety of medicines. This includes the reporting of ADRs by healthcare professionals, patients, and pharmaceutical companies. The information collected is analyzed, and any safety concerns are addressed through regulatory action, such as product labeling changes or drug withdrawals.

Case Studies:

The importance of ADR detection and reporting can be seen in several case studies. One such example is the case of thalidomide, a drug that was used to treat morning sickness in pregnant women in the 1950s and 1960s. It was later discovered that thalidomide caused severe birth defects, including missing or malformed limbs, in newborns. The tragedy led to increased regulatory oversight and the establishment of pharmacovigilance systems worldwide.

Another example is the case of rofecoxib (Vioxx), as mentioned earlier. The drug was approved in 1999 for the treatment of pain and inflammation but was withdrawn from the market in 2004 due to an increased risk of heart attacks and strokes. The withdrawal of Vioxx led to increased scrutiny of the drug approval process and the need for more extensive post-marketing surveillance.

ADR detection and reporting play a crucial role in ensuring patient safety and drug effectiveness. The potential consequences of undetected or underreported ADRs can be severe, leading to patient harm, disability, and even death. Pharmacovigilance activities, including the reporting of ADRs by healthcare professionals, patients, and pharmaceutical companies, are essential for identifying and minimizing risks associated with drug use. The continued expansion and improvement of pharmacovigilance systems will help to ensure that drugs are safe and effective for patients.

6.3 Methods for ADR detection

Adverse drug reactions (ADRs) are a significant concern for patient safety and can have serious consequences if left undetected or untreated. Therefore, it is important to have reliable methods for detecting and reporting ADRs. There are various methods available for detecting ADRs, including spontaneous reporting, cohort event monitoring, intensive monitoring, prescription-event monitoring, electronic health records, and clinical trials. Each method has its own strengths and limitations, and combining them can improve ADR detection and minimize harm to patients.

6.3.1 Spontaneous reporting

Adverse drug reactions (ADRs) can cause significant harm to patients and can even lead to death. Therefore, it is important to identify and prevent them as early as possible. Spontaneous reporting is the most common method used to detect ADRs. This method relies on healthcare professionals and patients reporting suspected ADRs to national pharmacovigilance centers. However, there are several limitations to this method.

One of the biggest limitations is underreporting. Since reporting ADRs is voluntary, it is estimated that only 10-20% of all ADRs are reported through spontaneous reporting systems. This underreporting can be due to a variety of reasons, including lack of awareness among healthcare professionals, fear of litigation, or lack of time. The underreporting of ADRs was evident in the case of rofecoxib (Vioxx), a nonsteroidal anti-inflammatory drug that was widely used to treat pain and inflammation. The drug was withdrawn from the market in 2004 after it was found to increase the risk of cardiovascular events such as heart attack and stroke. However, it was later revealed that the ADR had been reported as early as 2000, but it took several years for the signal to be detected due to underreporting.

Another limitation of spontaneous reporting is the lack of completeness and accuracy of the reported data. Healthcare professionals may not provide all the necessary information regarding the ADR, such as the dose, frequency, and duration of drug use, or the patient's medical history. This can make it difficult to assess the severity and preventability of the ADR, as well as to identify potential risk factors. Moreover, the reporting bias can also affect the accuracy of the data. Some ADRs may be overreported due to media attention, while others may be underreported due to their rarity.

Despite these limitations, spontaneous reporting remains a valuable tool for ADR detection and signal detection. National pharmacovigilance centers can use the reported data to identify new ADRs or patterns of ADRs associated with a particular drug or drug class. They can also use the data to assess the preventability and predictability of ADRs, which can help in developing preventive measures or modifying the drug label. For example, in the case of the antipsychotic drug olanzapine, the reporting of ADRs such as weight gain and metabolic disturbances led to the inclusion of a warning in the drug label regarding these potential adverse effects.

Spontaneous reporting is a cost-effective and easy-to-use method for ADR detection and signal detection. However, it has several limitations, such as underreporting and incomplete data, which can affect the accuracy and usefulness of the reported data. Therefore, efforts should be made to increase awareness among healthcare professionals and patients about the importance of reporting ADRs and to improve the completeness and accuracy of the reported data. In addition, other methods such as electronic health records and data mining can be used in conjunction with spontaneous reporting to improve ADR detection and signal detection.

6.3.2 Cohort event monitoring (CEM)

Cohort event monitoring (CEM) is a pharmacovigilance method that aims to identify previously unknown adverse drug reactions (ADRs) associated with a particular drug. It involves the collection of data on a cohort of patients who have been prescribed the drug of interest and are followed up over a period of time to identify any ADRs that may occur.

CEM is typically conducted in a prospective manner, meaning that patients are enrolled into the cohort at the time of starting the drug and are followed up for a specified period of time to detect any ADRs. The cohort is usually compared to a control group of patients who have not been exposed to the drug to identify any differences in the incidence of ADRs between the two groups.

CEM has several advantages over other pharmacovigilance methods. Firstly, it allows for the detection of rare and previously unknown ADRs, as the sample size is typically larger than in spontaneous reporting. Secondly, it allows for the estimation of incidence rates of ADRs, which can be used to inform the risk-benefit profile of the drug. Finally, it can provide more detailed information on the characteristics of the ADRs, such as the time of onset and severity.

One example of the successful use of CEM is in the monitoring of the use of isotretinoin, a drug used in the treatment of severe acne. CEM studies have identified several previously unknown ADRs associated with the drug, including depression, suicidal ideation, and inflammatory bowel disease. These findings led to changes in the drug label and prescribing guidelines to improve patient safety.

However, CEM also has some limitations. Firstly, it is a resource-intensive method that requires a large sample size and long-term follow-up. Secondly, there may be confounding factors that can affect the incidence of ADRs, such as the underlying disease and other concomitant medications. Finally, the cohort may not be representative of the general population, as patients may be excluded due to comorbidities or other factors.

Cohort event monitoring is a useful pharmacovigilance method that allows for the detection of previously unknown ADRs associated with a particular drug. It has been successfully used to improve patient safety in several instances and can provide valuable information on the risk-benefit profile of drugs. However, it is not without limitations and requires careful consideration of the study design and analysis to ensure valid results.

6.3.3 Intensive monitoring

Intensive monitoringalso known as active surveillance, is a pharmacovigilance approach that involves actively monitoring patients who have been prescribed a particular drug or are receiving a certain medical treatment. This approach is used to detect adverse drug reactions (ADRs) that may not have been identified through spontaneous reporting or other passive surveillance methods.

Intensive monitoring typically involves monitoring patients through a variety of methods, such as regular physical examinations, laboratory tests, and patient interviews. This method allows healthcare professionals to detect ADRs that may be difficult to identify through other methods, such as mild or asymptomatic events. Intensive monitoring is often used for high-risk drugs or in situations where a new drug is being introduced to the market.

One example of intensive monitoring is the use of pregnancy registries to monitor the safety of drugs during pregnancy. These registries collect information from pregnant women who are taking a particular drug or have been exposed to a drug during pregnancy. This information is then analyzed to determine if there is an increased risk of adverse events or birth defects associated with the drug.

Another example of intensive monitoring is the use of vaccine safety surveillance systems, which are used to monitor the safety of vaccines. These systems collect information from healthcare providers and patients about adverse events following vaccination. This information is then analyzed to determine if there are any safety concerns associated with the vaccine.

Intensive monitoring can also be used in clinical trials to monitor the safety of drugs during development. In these trials, patients are closely monitored for adverse events, and the data is analyzed to determine the safety and effectiveness of the drug.

Intensive monitoring is an important tool in pharmacovigilance that allows for the early detection of ADRs and can help improve patient safety. However, it can be resource-intensive and may not be feasible for all drugs or populations.

6.3.4 Prescription-event monitoring (PEM)

Prescription-event monitoring (PEM) is a pharmacovigilance technique used to detect and monitor adverse drug reactions (ADRs) associated with newly marketed drugs. It is a form of active surveillance where a sample of patients prescribed a specific drug is followed up for a period of time to detect any ADRs that occur. The method was first introduced in the United Kingdom in the 1980s and has since been used in many countries around the world.

The process of PEM involves identifying a cohort of patients who have been prescribed the drug of interest and collecting information about their demographics, medical history, and concomitant medications. The patients are then monitored for a period of time, usually six months to a year, and any suspected ADRs are recorded. The data is collected using a standardized form, which is sent to the regulatory authority responsible for pharmacovigilance.

PEM has several advantages over other pharmacovigilance methods. Firstly, it allows for the detection of rare and serious ADRs that may not have been detected in pre-marketing clinical trials. Secondly, it provides more detailed information about the incidence and characteristics of ADRs, which can be used to inform drug labeling and clinical practice. Finally, it allows for the early detection of ADRs, which can lead to timely regulatory action, such as drug withdrawal or label changes.

However, PEM also has some limitations. The method is resource-intensive and can be expensive to implement, particularly in large populations. Additionally, the sample size may not be representative of the wider population, leading to bias and potential limitations in generalizability. Finally, the method relies on the willingness of healthcare professionals to report suspected ADRs, which may be influenced by factors such as time constraints and lack of awareness.

Despite these limitations, PEM remains an important pharmacovigilance tool and has contributed to the detection and monitoring of many important ADRs. For example, PEM was used to detect the association between sodium valproate and neural tube defects in the offspring of women taking the drug during pregnancy, which led to changes in drug labeling and prescribing guidelines.

6.3.5 Electronic Health Records (EHRs)

Electronic Health Records (EHRs) are digital records of a patient's health information, including medical history, diagnoses, medications, and treatment plans. EHRs have become increasingly popular in recent years, as they allow healthcare providers to access and share patient data more easily, which can improve patient safety and quality of care.

EHRs can also be used for pharmacovigilance purposes, including ADR detection and monitoring. One advantage of using EHRs for pharmacovigilance is that they contain comprehensive data on patients' medical histories and medication use, making it easier to identify potential ADRs and assess their severity and impact. EHRs can also be used to monitor medication adherence and track outcomes over time.

There are, however, some limitations to using EHRs for pharmacovigilance. First, not all patients have access to EHRs, which can lead to underreporting of ADRs in certain populations.

Additionally, EHRs may contain incomplete or inaccurate information, which can make it difficult to assess the causality of an ADR or track its outcomes accurately. Finally, there may be privacy concerns associated with sharing EHR data for pharmacovigilance purposes, which must be addressed to ensure patient confidentiality and data security.

6.3.6. Clinical trials

Clinical trials are an essential tool in the development and approval of new drugs. During clinical trials, researchers monitor patients for ADRs to evaluate the safety and efficacy of the drug. The data collected during clinical trials are used to determine whether a drug should be approved for use, and if so, what warning labels and precautions should be included in the prescribing information.

Clinical trials involve a group of patients who are selected based on specific inclusion and exclusion criteria. These criteria ensure that the patients who participate in the study are representative of the patient population for which the drug is intended. The patients are then randomized into treatment and control groups. The treatment group receives the drug being tested, while the control group receives a placebo or an existing standard treatment.

The safety of the drug is monitored during the trial period, which may range from a few weeks to several years, depending on the drug's intended use. Adverse events are reported by the patients or healthcare professionals and recorded in the trial database. The data are then analyzed to determine the incidence and severity of ADRs in the treatment and control groups.

Clinical trials are useful in detecting ADRs in a controlled environment, where patients are carefully monitored and data collection is standardized. However, the sample size may be limited, and the data may not be representative of the general population. Additionally, some ADRs may not be detected during the clinical trial period, as they may not manifest until after the trial is completed, or in a larger patient population.

One example of a drug whose ADRs were not detected during clinical trials is rofecoxib (Vioxx). Vioxx was a non-steroidal anti-inflammatory drug (NSAID) that was approved for use in 1999. Clinical trials showed that Vioxx was effective in treating pain and inflammation, and that it had a lower risk of gastrointestinal bleeding than other NSAIDs. However, in 2004, Vioxx was withdrawn from the market due to an increased risk of cardiovascular events, such as heart attack and stroke. The increased risk of cardiovascular events was not detected during the clinical trials, but was revealed after the drug had been on the market for several years and had been used by millions of patients.

Another example is the case of thalidomide, a drug that was developed in the 1950s to treat morning sickness in pregnant women. Thalidomide was approved for use in many countries based on limited clinical trial data, and it was estimated that around 10,000 children were born with birth defects as a result of their mothers taking the drug during pregnancy. Thalidomide was subsequently withdrawn from the market and stricter regulations were implemented for drug approval and safety monitoring.

Clinical trials are an important method for ADR detection and safety evaluation. However, their limitations must be recognized, and other methods of ADR detection and monitoring, such as spontaneous reporting, intensive monitoring, and electronic health records, should be used in conjunction with clinical trials to ensure that the safety of drugs is monitored throughout their lifecycle.

6.4 Factors affecting ADR reporting:

Adverse drug reaction (ADR) reporting is a critical aspect of pharmacovigilance that enables the detection and assessment of the safety of drugs in real-world settings. However, several factors can influence the reporting of ADRs, including healthcare professional knowledge and attitudes, patient awareness and willingness to report, and regulatory requirements. Understanding these factors and addressing them can help to improve ADR reporting rates and enhance drug safety.

6.4.1 Healthcare professional knowledge and attitudes

Adverse drug reactions (ADRs) are a major public health concern, as they can cause significant morbidity and mortality. Effective ADR reporting is essential for the identification and management of drug safety issues. However, ADR reporting rates are often low, and the factors that influence reporting behavior are complex. One of the key factors affecting ADR reporting is healthcare professional knowledge and attitudes.

Healthcare professionals (HCPs) are the primary source of ADR reports, as they are responsible for monitoring patients for ADRs and reporting suspected events to the relevant regulatory authorities. However, HCPs may be reluctant to report ADRs for a variety of reasons. One of the most important factors is their level of knowledge and understanding of ADRs and the reporting process.

Several studies have shown that lack of awareness and knowledge of pharmacovigilance principles, as well as negative attitudes towards reporting, can result in underreporting of ADRs. For instance, a study conducted in Egypt found that only 20% of HCPs were aware of the national pharmacovigilance system, and only 7% had reported an ADR in the past. Similarly, a survey of Australian HCPs revealed that only 11% of respondents had reported an ADR in the past, with lack of time and perceived complexity of the reporting process cited as the main barriers.Studies have shown that many HCPs have a poor understanding of ADRs, including their incidence, severity, and impact on patient outcomes. This lack of knowledge can lead to underreporting of ADRs, as HCPs may not recognize or attribute ADRs correctly. For example, a study of ADR reporting by nurses found that many were not familiar with the concept of a "serious" ADR and did not report events that did not result in hospitalization or death.

In addition to knowledge gaps, HCP attitudes towards ADR reporting can also affect reporting rates. Fear of legal and professional repercussions is a common concern, with HCPs worried that reporting ADRs may damage their reputation or result in litigation. A lack of feedback on the outcome of ADR reports can also be demotivating for HCPs, who may feel that their reports are not making a difference.

To address these issues, several strategies can be employed to improve HCP knowledge and attitudes towards ADR reporting. These include providing regular training and education on pharmacovigilance principles, simplifying the reporting process, and providing feedback on the outcome of ADR reports. For example, a study conducted in Saudi Arabia found that providing HCPs with regular training on pharmacovigilance principles led to a significant increase in ADR reporting rates.

6.4.2 Patient awareness and willingness to report ADRs

Patient awareness and willingness to report ADRs is an essential aspect of pharmacovigilance. Patients are often the first to experience ADRs and can provide valuable information to healthcare professionals regarding drug safety. However, patients may not always be aware of ADRs and may not report them to their healthcare providers. This lack of reporting can lead to underreporting of ADRs and delay in detecting potential safety issues.For example, a survey of patients in Nigeria found that only 10% had ever reported an ADR, with lack of awareness and fear of negative consequences cited as the main barriers.

One of the main reasons for the lack of patient reporting is the lack of awareness of ADRs. Patients may not be familiar with the concept of ADRs and may not know what to look out for. Moreover, patients may not realize that the symptoms they are experiencing could be related to the medication they are taking. In some cases, patients may attribute their symptoms to other factors such as stress or aging, which can lead to underreporting of ADRs.

Another factor that affects patient reporting is the fear of the unknown. Patients may be afraid of the potential consequences of reporting an ADR, such as having to stop taking the medication or being prescribed a different drug. Additionally, patients may be worried about being labeled as "difficult" or "complaining," which can discourage them from reporting ADRs.

Furthermore, patients may not be aware of how to report ADRs and may not know whom to contact. The process of reporting ADRs can be confusing and time-consuming, which can discourage patients from reporting. Patients may also assume that their healthcare provider is responsible for reporting ADRs and may not realize that they can also report ADRs themselves.

To address these issues, efforts have been made to increase patient awareness and education regarding ADRs. Patient education campaigns have been conducted to increase awareness of ADRs and to encourage patients to report any suspected ADRs to their healthcare providers. For example, the Food and Drug Administration (FDA) in the United States has launched the MedWatch program, which is a national reporting system for ADRs. The program provides information to patients on how to report ADRs and encourages them to report any suspected ADRs to the FDA.Similarly , a study conducted in the United Kingdom found that providing patients with an easy-to-use ADR reporting system led to a significant increase in ADR reporting rates.

Moreover, healthcare providers play a vital role in promoting patient reporting of ADRs. They can educate their patients about the importance of reporting ADRs and encourage them to report any suspected ADRs promptly. Additionally, healthcare providers can make the reporting process more accessible and straightforward for patients, such as providing them with written instructions or directing them to resources such as MedWatch.

Patient awareness and willingness to report ADRs are crucial in ensuring drug safety. Patients play an essential role in detecting potential ADRs and can provide valuable information to healthcare providers regarding drug safety. Efforts should be made to increase patient awareness of ADRs and to encourage them to report any suspected ADRs promptly. Healthcare providers should also play an active role in promoting patient reporting of ADRs and making the reporting process more accessible for patients. By working together, patients and healthcare providers can improve drug safety and enhance pharmacovigilance efforts.

6.4.3 Regulatory requirements

Regulatory requirements play a significant role in influencing ADR reporting rates. Inadequate regulatory requirements may lead to poor ADR reporting rates and may compromise patient safety. However, regulatory bodies can take several measures to improve ADR reporting rates and ensure better patient safety.

For example, a study conducted in Iran found that only 19% of ADRs were reported to the national pharmacovigilance system, with lack of awareness and fear of legal consequences cited as the main barriers. Similarly, a study conducted in the European Union found that regulatory requirements may not be sufficient to ensure adequate ADR reporting, with underreporting and poor data quality cited as significant concerns.

To address these issues, regulatory bodies can take several steps to improve ADR reporting rates. One way to do this is by simplifying reporting requirements, making it easier for healthcare professionals and patients to report ADRs. Simplified reporting requirements can also help reduce the burden on healthcare professionals and improve compliance rates.

Providing incentives for reporting is another way to improve ADR reporting rates. Financial incentives, such as payments for each ADR report, can motivate healthcare professionals to report ADRs promptly. The European Medicines Agency (EMA) has implemented financial incentives for reporting, which has resulted in a significant increase in ADR reporting rates.

Improving data quality through data mining and signal detection is another way to improve ADR reporting rates. By using data mining and signal detection techniques, regulatory bodies can identify potential ADRs and take action to prevent further harm to patients. The EMA has implemented data mining and signal detection techniques to improve data quality and identify potential ADRs.

Regulatory requirements play a critical role in influencing ADR reporting rates. Inadequate regulatory requirements may lead to poor ADR reporting rates, compromising patient safety. However, regulatory bodies can take several measures to improve ADR reporting rates, including simplifying reporting requirements, providing incentives for reporting, and improving data quality through data mining and signal detection techniques. These measures can help ensure better patient safety and improve the overall quality of healthcare.

6.5 Pharmacovigilance systems

Pharmacovigilance (PV) is the science and activities related to the detection, assessment, understanding, and prevention of adverse effects or any other drug-related problem. The primary goal of a pharmacovigilance system is to ensure patient safety by identifying and managing adverse drug reactions (ADRs) associated with the use of medicines. A comprehensive pharmacovigilance system involves multiple stakeholders, including national regulatory authorities, drug manufacturers, healthcare professionals, and patients.

National regulatory authorities (NRAs) are responsible for ensuring the safety, efficacy, and quality of medicines. NRAs play a crucial role in the pharmacovigilance system by monitoring the safety of medicines in their respective countries. They are responsible for reviewing drug applications, approving new drugs, and ensuring that the approved drugs are used safely. NRAs also oversee the reporting of adverse drug reactions by healthcare professionals and drug manufacturers and take appropriate regulatory action when necessary.

Drug manufacturers have a responsibility to monitor the safety of their products throughout the product's life cycle, from development to post-marketing. They are required to report all adverse events associated with their products to the NRAs. In addition to reporting ADRs, drug manufacturers are also responsible for conducting post-marketing surveillance studies to monitor the safety of their products.

Healthcare professionals are key players in the pharmacovigilance system, as they are the first line of defense in detecting and reporting ADRs. They are responsible for identifying and managing adverse drug reactions in their patients and reporting them to the appropriate regulatory authority. Healthcare professionals can also contribute to the pharmacovigilance system by providing feedback on the safety and efficacy of medicines to drug manufacturers and regulatory authorities.

Patients also have an important role in the pharmacovigilance system, as they are the end-users of medicines. Patients can provide valuable information on the safety and efficacy of medicines by reporting any adverse effects they experience while taking their medications. Patient reporting can help detect previously unknown or rare ADRs and contribute to improving the overall safety of medicines.

Effective collaboration and communication among stakeholders are essential to ensure the success of a pharmacovigilance system. Collaboration between NRAs, drug manufacturers, healthcare professionals, and patients can lead to the early detection of ADRs and the implementation of appropriate measures to prevent harm to patients. For example, the European Medicines Agency (EMA) established the Pharmacovigilance Risk Assessment Committee (PRAC), which includes members from regulatory authorities, healthcare professionals, and patient organizations, to evaluate safety signals and make recommendations for regulatory action.

Thus, a pharmacovigilance system involves multiple stakeholders, each with their roles and responsibilities in detecting and reporting adverse drug reactions. Effective collaboration and communication between stakeholders are essential to ensure the safety of medicines and prevent harm to patients.

6.6 Adverse Event Management: From Detection to Resolution

Adverse drug reactions (ADRs) can have significant impacts on patients, ranging from mild symptoms to serious harm and even death. Effective management of ADRs requires a systematic approach that starts with their detection and reporting, and continues through follow-up and resolution. Pharmacovigilance plays a crucial role in identifying safety concerns and ensuring the safety of patients.

The first step in ADR management is detecting and reporting the event. Healthcare professionals, patients, and drug manufacturers can all report suspected ADRs to national regulatory authorities, such as the Pharmacovigilance Programme of India (PvPI). Accurate and complete reporting is crucial to identifying safety concerns and taking appropriate actions to mitigate risks.

After an ADR is reported, it is evaluated to determine its causality, severity, and preventability. Causality assessment involves determining the likelihood that the drug caused the ADR, using tools such as the World Health Organization-Uppsala Monitoring Centre (WHO-UMC) causality assessment system. Severity assessment involves determining the severity of the ADR using established scales such as the Common Terminology Criteria for Adverse Events (CTCAE). Preventability assessment involves evaluating whether the ADR could have been avoided, using tools such as the Schumock and Thornton preventability scale.

Once the causality, severity, and preventability of the ADR are determined, appropriate actions can be taken to manage the event. In cases where the ADR is mild or moderate, the drug may be continued with monitoring and supportive care. In more severe cases, the drug may need to be discontinued or its dose reduced, and additional medical interventions may be necessary.

Follow-up and monitoring of the patient is essential in managing ADRs. This involves regular monitoring of the patient's symptoms and laboratory values, as well as communication with the patient to ensure they understand the risks and benefits of their treatment. Patient education is also important in empowering patients to report any new symptoms or changes in their health status.

In addition to managing individual ADRs, pharmacovigilance plays a critical role in identifying and addressing safety concerns at the population level. This includes ongoing monitoring of drug safety using data from spontaneous reporting, electronic health records, and other sources. In some cases, additional studies such as post-marketing surveillance studies or clinical trials may be needed to further evaluate the safety of a drug.

Effective management of ADRs requires a comprehensive approach that involves detection, reporting, causality assessment, severity assessment, preventability assessment, and appropriate management and follow-up. Accurate and complete reporting is crucial to identifying safety concerns and taking appropriate actions to mitigate risks. Pharmacovigilance plays a crucial role in ensuring the safety of patients, both at the individual and population levels.

6.7 Challenges and future directions

Adverse drug reactions (ADRs) are a significant public health issue that can result in serious harm or even death if not detected and managed promptly. Despite the importance of ADR detection and reporting, there are several challenges that limit the effectiveness of current pharmacovigilance systems. In this essay, we will discuss the challenges facing ADR detection and reporting and identify potential solutions and future directions for improving ADR detection and reporting.

One of the most significant challenges facing ADR detection and reporting is underreporting. Healthcare professionals may fail to report ADRs due to a lack of awareness or training, fear of legal or professional repercussions, or a perception that the ADR is not serious enough to warrant reporting. Patients may also be reluctant to report ADRs due to a lack of knowledge or awareness of reporting mechanisms, fear of negative consequences, or a belief that the ADR is a normal part of treatment. Underreporting can result in a failure to detect and address safety concerns, potentially leading to harm or even death.

Another challenge facing ADR detection and reporting is resource constraints. Many pharmacovigilance systems, particularly in low- and middle-income countries, lack the resources and expertise necessary to conduct effective ADR monitoring and reporting. This can result in incomplete or inaccurate data, which can compromise the ability of regulatory authorities to make informed decisions regarding drug safety.

To address these challenges, several potential solutions and future directions have been proposed. One solution is the use of new technologies to improve ADR detection and reporting. For example, electronic health records (EHRs) can be used to automatically detect potential ADRs and prompt healthcare professionals to report them. Additionally, social media platforms and mobile applications can be used to collect ADR data directly from patients, increasing the completeness and timeliness of reporting.

Another potential solution is increased patient involvement in ADR detection and reporting. Patients can play a critical role in detecting and reporting ADRs, particularly those that are rare or long-term. However, patient reporting systems must be accessible and easy to use, and patients must be educated on the importance of reporting ADRs.

Finally, improved regulatory oversight is critical for ensuring the effectiveness of pharmacovigilance systems. Regulatory authorities must have the resources and expertise necessary to analyze and act on ADR data effectively. Additionally, regulatory authorities must work closely with other stakeholders, including drug manufacturers, healthcare professionals, and patients, to identify and address safety concerns.

ADR detection and reporting is critical for ensuring drug safety and protecting public health. However, several challenges, including underreporting and resource constraints, limit the effectiveness of current pharmacovigilance systems. To address these challenges, potential solutions include the use of new technologies, increased patient involvement, and improved regulatory oversight. By working together to overcome these challenges, we can ensure that ADRs are detected and managed promptly, improving patient outcomes and reducing the burden of harm caused by ADRs.

VII
Methods in Causality Assessment

Causality assessment is the process of evaluating the relationship between an adverse event and a suspected drug or medication. It involves determining the likelihood that the drug caused the adverse event, based on available data such as medical history, clinical examination, laboratory tests, and drug exposure information. The goal of causality assessment is to establish whether the suspected drug or medication is the cause of the adverse event, and to determine the strength of the association between the two.

Causality assessment is an essential part of pharmacovigilance, which is the science and activities related to the detection, assessment, understanding, and prevention of adverse effects or any other drug-related problems. It is important to perform causality assessment to ensure patient safety and improve drug regulation. Inadequate causality assessment can lead to the approval and continued use of drugs that cause serious adverse events, which can result in patient harm and even death.

7.1 Methods in Causality assessment

There are various types of causality assessment methods, including probabilistic approaches, expert-based approaches, and algorithmic approaches.

7.1.1 Probabilistic approaches

Probabilistic approaches involve using algorithms or scoring systems to assign a probability score to the relationship between a drug and an adverse event. One such approach is the Naranjo algorithm, which is a widely used tool for causality assessment.

A. Naranjo algorithm

The Naranjo algorithm is a widely used tool for the assessment of the causality of adverse drug reactions (ADRs). It was developed by Dr. Cesar Naranjo in 1981 and has since been widely adopted in pharmacovigilance and clinical research settings.The Naranjo algorithm uses a series of questions to evaluate the likelihood of a causal relationship between a drug and an adverse event. The questions cover factors such as the timing of the adverse event in relation to drug administration, the presence of other possible causes, and the effect of dechallenge and rechallenge.

The Naranjo algorithm is a 10-item questionnaire that assigns a score to each item based on the information provided by the patient or healthcare provider. The score for each item ranges from -1 to +2, with higher scores indicating a greater likelihood that the adverse event was caused by the drug in question. The total score ranges from -4 to +13, with a score of 0 indicating an uncertain relationship between the drug and the adverse event.

The items in the Naranjo algorithm questionnaire include factors such as the temporal relationship between drug administration and the onset of the adverse event, the presence of other risk factors or co-morbidities, the likelihood of the adverse event occurring with other drugs in the same class, and the response to dechallenge or rechallenge with the drug in question.

The Naranjo algorithm has been shown to be a reliable and valid tool for the assessment of ADR causality in a variety of clinical settings. However, it is not without its limitations. One limitation is that it relies heavily on subjective judgments and may be influenced by factors such as bias or incomplete information. Additionally, the Naranjo algorithm does not take into account the severity of the adverse event, which can be an important factor in determining causality.

Despite these limitations, the Naranjo algorithm remains a widely used tool for ADR causality assessment. Its simplicity and ease of use make it a valuable tool for healthcare providers and researchers alike.

B. Liverpool Causality Assessment Tool

The Liverpool Causality Assessment Tool (LCAT) is a tool used to assess the causality of adverse drug reactions (ADRs). It was developed in 1993 by a team of researchers at the University of Liverpool, UK, and is one of the most widely used causality assessment tools in clinical practice and research.

The LCAT is based on the principle that the probability of an ADR being caused by a drug increases if the ADR occurs shortly after the initiation of treatment, if the ADR disappears or improves upon discontinuation of the drug, and if the ADR recurs upon re-exposure to the drug. The LCAT consists of six categories, each of which assesses a different aspect of causality, and assigns a numerical score ranging from -2 to +2 based on the likelihood of a causal relationship between the drug and the ADR.

The six categories of the LCAT are:

Time to Onset: This category assesses the time interval between the initiation of the drug and the onset of the ADR. A shorter time interval is indicative of a higher likelihood of a causal relationship.

Course of the Adverse Event: This category assesses the severity and duration of the ADR. A severe and prolonged ADR is indicative of a higher likelihood of a causal relationship.

Dechallenge: This category assesses whether the ADR disappeared or improved upon discontinuation of the drug. If the ADR disappeared or improved, it is indicative of a higher likelihood of a causal relationship.

Rechallenge: This category assesses whether the ADR recurred upon re-exposure to the drug. If the ADR recurred, it is indicative of a higher likelihood of a causal relationship.

Previous Information on the Drug: This category assesses whether there is any known information about the drug causing similar ADRs in the past. If there is, it is indicative of a higher likelihood of a causal relationship.

Concomitant Medication and Disease: This category assesses whether the ADR could be due to a concomitant medication or underlying disease. If there is no alternative explanation, it is indicative of a higher likelihood of a causal relationship.

The scores assigned to each category are then added up to give an overall score, which ranges from -4 to +12. A score of +6 or higher indicates a "probable" or "highly probable" causal relationship between the drug and the ADR, while a score of -2 or lower indicates an "unlikely" or "excluded" causal relationship.

The LCAT has been used in a wide range of clinical settings and has been found to be a reliable and valid tool for assessing causality of ADRs. However, like all causality assessment tools, it has some limitations, such as subjectivity in assigning scores and the potential for missing important confounding factors.

C. Bayesian analysis

Bayesian analysis is a statistical method used to estimate the probability of an event or hypothesis based on prior knowledge and evidence. It is named after Thomas Bayes, an 18th-century English statistician and philosopher who first formulated Bayes' theorem.

In Bayesian analysis, the prior probability of an event is updated based on new data or evidence, resulting in a posterior probability. This method is particularly useful when dealing with uncertain or incomplete data, as it allows for the incorporation of prior knowledge and the updating of probabilities as new information becomes available.

Bayesian analysis has a wide range of applications in various fields, including medicine, engineering, finance, and social sciences. In medicine, for example, it can be used to assess the effectiveness and safety of drugs or medical interventions by combining data from clinical trials with prior knowledge of the disease and treatment. Bayesian analysis can also be used in risk assessment and decision-making processes, such as in environmental risk assessment or in assessing the reliability of complex systems.

One of the advantages of Bayesian analysis is that it provides a clear framework for incorporating prior knowledge and assumptions, which can help to reduce uncertainty and bias in statistical analysis. However, one of the challenges of Bayesian analysis is that it can be computationally intensive, particularly when dealing with large datasets or complex models.

Overall, Bayesian analysis is a powerful tool for analyzing complex data and making informed decisions based on uncertain or incomplete information. Its versatility and flexibility make it a valuable tool in a wide range of fields, and it continues to be an active area of research and development in statistical methodology.

D. The Roussel Uclaf Causality Assessment Method (RUCAM)

The Roussel Uclaf Causality Assessment Method (RUCAM) is a structured, quantitative method for assessing the likelihood that an adverse drug reaction (ADR) is caused by a specific medication. Developed in the 1980s by the Roussel Uclaf pharmaceutical company and now maintained by the Council for International Organizations of Medical Sciences (CIOMS), RUCAM provides a systematic approach to causality assessment that takes into account the temporal relationship between the drug and the event, the known or expected pharmacological effects of the drug, and the absence of other plausible explanations for the event.

RUCAM consists of a series of seven questions that are scored based on the available evidence for each question. The questions cover factors such as the time to onset of the event, the presence of alternative causes, the likelihood of the event being due to chance, and the ability of the drug to cause the event based on its known pharmacological effects. The total score is then used to assign a category of causality, ranging from "definite" to "unlikely," with intermediate categories for "probable," "possible," and "conditional" causality.

RUCAM has been widely used in pharmacovigilance and clinical research as a standardized method for assessing causality in suspected ADRs. It has been validated in numerous studies and is considered one of the most reliable and consistent methods for causality assessment. However, like other methods, RUCAM is not without limitations. It relies heavily on the quality and completeness of the available data and may not capture all possible causes or confounding factors. Additionally, the scoring system can be subjective and may vary depending on the experience and training of the assessor.

Overall, the Roussel Uclaf Causality Assessment Method provides a standardized and systematic approach to assessing causality in suspected ADRs. It can be a valuable tool for pharmacovigilance and clinical research, but it should be used in conjunction with other methods and clinical judgment to ensure accurate and comprehensive assessment of causality.

7.1.2 Expert-based approaches

A. Clinical judgement method

The clinical judgement method is an expert-based approach for causality assessment that relies on the experience and expertise of healthcare professionals to determine the likelihood of a drug causing an adverse event. In this method, the clinician considers factors such as the temporal relationship between drug administration and onset of the adverse event, the plausibility of the event being caused by the drug, and any other factors that may contribute to the event.

Clinical judgement is commonly used in situations where other causality assessment methods cannot be applied, such as in single-patient cases or when the patient has multiple comorbidities or is taking multiple medications. It can also be used in combination with other methods to increase the accuracy of the assessment.

The strengths of the clinical judgement method include its flexibility and adaptability to individual cases, the ability to consider all relevant factors, and the reliance on expert knowledge and experience. However, the method is also subject to individual biases and can be affected by factors such as the clinician's knowledge, training, and experience.

Overall, the clinical judgement method is a valuable tool for causality assessment and can provide important insights into the likelihood of a drug causing an adverse event in individual patients. However, it should be used in combination with other methods and its limitations should be carefully considered.

B. Karch and Lasagna Criteria

The Karch and Lasagna Criteria is a set of causality assessment criteria developed by Karch and Lasagna in 1975. This approach uses a scoring system to assess the probability that an adverse event is related to a drug. The criteria take into account the temporal relationship between drug administration and the onset of symptoms, the presence of alternative explanations for the event, and the known pharmacological actions of the drug.

The Karch and Lasagna Criteria involve a total of eight questions that are used to evaluate the relationship between a drug and an adverse event. The questions cover a range of factors including the temporal relationship between the drug and the event, the effect of dose changes, the presence of alternative explanations, the patient's medical history, and the known pharmacological actions of the drug.

Each question is assigned a score of 0, 1, or 2 based on the degree of evidence supporting the relationship between the drug and the event. The scores are then totaled, and the total score is used to classify the relationship as definite, probable, possible, or doubtful.

The Karch and Lasagna Criteria have been used in a variety of settings to assess the causality of adverse events. One study used the criteria to evaluate adverse drug reactions in hospitalized patients, finding that the criteria had a high level of agreement with expert opinion.

However, the Karch and Lasagna Criteria have also been criticized for being subjective and difficult to apply consistently. In addition, the criteria do not take into account the severity of the adverse event or the potential impact on the patient's health.

As such, they are often used in conjunction with other causality assessment methods to provide a more comprehensive evaluation of adverse events.

C. Kramer's Criteria

Kramer's criteria is an expert-based approach used for the assessment of causality between a suspected drug and an adverse event. It was first proposed by Kramer in 1963 and has since been modified and updated by various researchers. The criteria involve a series of questions to be answered by a panel of experts to determine the likelihood of a causal relationship between a drug and an adverse event.

Kramer's criteria consist of three levels of causality: possible, probable, and definite. The levels are determined by the number of questions answered affirmatively by the expert panel. The questions include the temporal relationship between drug administration and the onset of the adverse event, the presence of other possible causes, the known pharmacological effects of the drug, the response to rechallenge, and the dechallenge effect.

While Kramer's criteria are widely used in clinical practice, they have some limitations. One limitation is that the criteria are subjective and depend on the expertise and experience of the expert panel. Another limitation is that they do not take into account the variability of individual patients and their response to drugs. Finally, the criteria do not provide a quantitative measure of the strength of the causal relationship between a drug and an adverse event.

Despite these limitations, Kramer's criteria remain an important tool for the assessment of causality between drugs and adverse events. They are used in pharmacovigilance and drug safety monitoring programs, and they provide a standardized and systematic approach to the evaluation of suspected adverse drug reactions.

D. The World Health Organization-Uppsala Monitoring Centre System

The World Health Organization-Uppsala Monitoring Centre (WHO-UMC) system is an expert-based approach to causality assessment of ADRs. The system was developed by the WHO and the Uppsala Monitoring Centre in 1978 to facilitate the global monitoring and reporting of adverse drug reactions.

The WHO-UMC system consists of six categories of causality assessment: certain, probable/likely, possible, unlikely, conditional/ unclassified, and unclassifiable. The system also includes three causality criteria: temporal relationship, dechallenge/rechallenge, and alternative causes.

To determine the category of causality, the system uses a set of guidelines based on the three causality criteria. For example, if the adverse event occurs shortly after drug administration and resolves after discontinuation of the drug, and there are no other possible causes for the event, the event may be classified as "certain". If there is a temporal relationship between the drug and the event but other causes cannot be ruled out, the event may be classified as "possible".

The WHO-UMC system is widely used in pharmacovigilance and is recommended by the WHO for causality assessment. It has been validated in several studies and has shown good inter-rater reliability. However, the system has some limitations, including subjectivity in interpretation and reliance on expert judgement.

The WHO-UMC system is a useful tool for assessing causality of ADRs, especially in the absence of definitive diagnostic tests or laboratory data. It provides a standardized approach to causality assessment and facilitates communication between healthcare professionals, regulatory authorities, and the pharmaceutical industry regarding drug safety.

7.1.3 Algorithmic approaches

A. Consensus-based Diagnostic System (CDS)

The Consensus-based Diagnostic System (CDS) is an algorithmic approach to causality assessment developed by a group of international experts in pharmacovigilance. The CDS was designed to provide a standardized and objective method for evaluating the causality of adverse drug reactions (ADRs) based on clinical and laboratory evidence.

The CDS uses a series of questions to guide the evaluator through the causality assessment process. These questions are organized into four categories: temporal relationship, dechallenge and rechallenge, alternative causes, and drug-related factors. Each question is assigned a score, and the scores are then tallied to determine the overall level of causality.

The CDS has been found to be a reliable and valid method for causality assessment, with good inter-rater agreement among evaluators. It has also been shown to be useful in identifying ADRs missed by other methods, such as spontaneous reporting.

One potential limitation of the CDS is that it relies heavily on clinical judgment and may be influenced by the evaluator's prior knowledge and experience. Additionally, some have criticized the CDS for being too complex and time-consuming, which may limit its practical utility in busy clinical settings.

B. The Council for International Organizations of Medical Sciences (CIOMS) Algorithm

The Council for International Organizations of Medical Sciences (CIOMS) Algorithm is a widely used method for assessing the causality of adverse drug reactions (ADRs). It was first published in 1985 by the Council for International Organizations of Medical Sciences, a non-profit organization that promotes the safe and effective use of medicines worldwide.

The CIOMS Algorithm is based on a set of nine criteria that are used to determine the likelihood that a particular drug caused a particular ADR. These criteria include the temporal relationship between the drug and the ADR, the pattern of the ADR, the response to re-challenge with the drug, and the presence of alternative explanations for the ADR.

Each criterion is assigned a score of 0, 1, or 2, depending on how well it is met. The scores are then added up to give a total score, which is used to classify the causality of the ADR as certain, probable, possible, unlikely, or unclassified.

One of the strengths of the CIOMS Algorithm is its flexibility. It can be used with both clinical trial and post-marketing data, and it can be adapted to different types of ADRs and drugs. It also takes into account alternative explanations for the ADR, which can help to prevent over-attribution of causality to the drug.

However, the CIOMS Algorithm is not without limitations. Some of the criteria, such as the response to re-challenge, may not always be applicable or feasible to use in practice. In addition, the algorithm relies on the judgment of the assessor, which can introduce subjectivity into the causality assessment.

The CIOMS Algorithm is a valuable tool for assessing the causality of ADRs, but it should be used in conjunction with other methods and with caution to ensure accurate and reliable results.

7.2 Challenges in Causality Assessment

Causality assessment is an essential aspect of pharmacovigilance, which involves the evaluation of the relationship between a drug and an adverse event. The accurate identification of drug-related adverse events is crucial for patient safety and the effective management of drug therapy. However, causality assessment is often challenging due to several factors that can affect the accuracy and consistency of the assessment.

A. Subjectivity of the assessment process

One of the major challenges in causality assessment is the subjectivity of the assessment process. Causality assessment relies heavily on clinical judgement, which can be influenced by various factors such as personal experience, knowledge, and bias. This subjectivity can lead to inconsistencies in the assessment, particularly when different assessors apply different criteria or interpret the same criteria differently.

B. Lack of standardization in the assessment process

There are currently several different causality assessment tools and algorithms available, each with its own set of criteria and scoring system. The lack of standardization can lead to confusion and inconsistency in the assessment process, particularly when different tools are used or when assessors apply different criteria.

C. Difficulty in detecting rare events

Rare adverse events may not be detected during clinical trials or may not be reported in post-marketing surveillance, which can make it difficult to establish a causal relationship between a drug and a rare adverse event. This can result in underreporting of adverse events, which can lead to delays in identifying and managing drug-related risks.

D. Limited information

Causality assessment relies heavily on the quality and completeness of available data, including patient medical histories, drug exposure information, and clinical findings. However, in many cases, the available information may be incomplete or of poor quality, making it difficult to accurately assess causality.

To address these challenges, efforts are being made to standardize and improve the causality assessment process. For example, the Council for International Organizations of Medical Sciences (CIOMS) has developed a standardized causality assessment algorithm that has been widely adopted by regulatory agencies and pharmaceutical companies. Additionally, the use of Bayesian analysis and other advanced statistical methods can help to improve the accuracy and consistency of causality assessments.

Causality assessment is an essential component of pharmacovigilance, but it is not without its challenges. The subjectivity of assessment, lack of standardization, difficulty in detecting rare events, and limited information can all affect the accuracy and consistency of causality assessments. Efforts to standardize and improve the assessment process, as well as the use of advanced statistical methods, can help to overcome these challenges and improve patient safety.

7.3 Future Directions in Causality Assessment

In recent years, there has been a growing interest in the use of machine learning and artificial intelligence (AI) for causality assessment. These technologies have the potential to improve the accuracy and efficiency of causality assessment by analyzing large amounts of data and identifying patterns that might not be immediately apparent to human assessors. For example, a study conducted by researchers at Stanford University used machine learning algorithms to identify potential adverse drug events from electronic health records (EHRs). The algorithms were able to identify previously unknown adverse events and to predict the likelihood of a particular adverse event occurring in a patient based on their medical history and other factors.

In addition to the use of machine learning and AI, there is a need for the development of standardized guidelines for causality assessment. While there are many different tools and algorithms available for causality assessment, there is currently no universally accepted standard for how causality assessment should be performed. This lack of standardization can lead to inconsistencies in how adverse events are assessed and reported, making it difficult to compare and analyze data across different studies and healthcare systems.

Improved data collection and analysis are also essential for improving causality assessment. This includes the collection of more complete and accurate information about patients, including their medical histories, medications, and other relevant factors. It also involves the use of advanced data analysis techniques to identify patterns and trends in adverse events, as well as to identify potential risk factors and other factors that may contribute to the occurrence of adverse events.

Finally, increased collaboration between stakeholders is essential for improving causality assessment. This includes collaboration between healthcare professionals, drug manufacturers, regulatory agencies, and patients. By working together, these stakeholders can share information and insights, identify potential adverse events more quickly, and develop more effective strategies for preventing and managing adverse events.

VIII

Severity and Seriousness assessment

8.1 Introduction

A. Definition of ADR Severity and Seriousness

Adverse drug reactions (ADRs) are harmful or unintended effects of medication that occur at normal therapeutic doses during clinical use. ADRs can range from mild and transient effects, such as nausea and vomiting, to severe and life-threatening events, such as anaphylaxis and organ failure. The severity of an ADR refers to the intensity and duration of the effect, while the seriousness of an ADR refers to the potential for harm or danger to the patient, including death, hospitalization, disability, or congenital malformations.

The severity of an ADR is typically categorized into grades based on the Common Terminology Criteria for Adverse Events (CTCAE), which provides a standardized approach to grading the severity of ADRs. CTCAE grades range from 1 to 5, with grade 1 being mild and grade 5 being fatal. The grades take into consideration the level of intervention required, duration of the reaction, and impact on daily activities.

The seriousness of an ADR is determined by regulatory authorities and is based on the potential consequences of the reaction, including death, hospitalization, disability, or congenital malformations. A serious ADR is one that results in any of the above outcomes or requires intervention to prevent such outcomes.

B. Importance of ADR Severity and Seriousness

Assessment of the severity and seriousness of ADRs is crucial in the management of drug therapy and the development of safe and effective medications. Understanding the severity of an ADR can guide healthcare professionals in deciding on appropriate treatment options and preventing further harm to the patient. For example, a severe ADR may require a change in medication or dose, while a mild ADR may only require symptomatic treatment.

On the other hand, assessing the seriousness of an ADR is important for regulatory authorities in determining the risk-benefit profile of a medication. The seriousness of an ADR is a key factor in determining whether a medication should be approved, withdrawn from the market, or have its label updated with additional warnings and precautions.

Moreover, assessing the severity and seriousness of ADRs can help in identifying potential drug-drug interactions, medication errors, and patient-specific factors that may increase the risk of ADRs. This information can be used to improve medication safety and prevent future harm to patients.

ADR severity and seriousness assessment is a critical component of pharmacovigilance and drug therapy management. Accurate and consistent assessment of ADRs can aid in improving patient outcomes, ensuring medication safety, and developing safe and effective medications.

8.2 Factors Influencing ADR Severity and Seriousness

8.2.1 Patient factors

Adverse drug reactions (ADRs) can range in severity from mild and self-limiting to life-threatening. The severity and seriousness of an ADR are determined by various factors, including patient-specific factors. Understanding patient factors that influence the severity and seriousness of ADRs is crucial for proper management and prevention of these events.

A. Age

Older adults are at higher risk for ADRs due to age related changes in metabolism and excretion of drugs, as well as increased prevalence of comorbidities and polypharmacy. Additionally, older adults may have decreased physiologic reserve, making them more vulnerable to severe ADRs. For example, a common side effect of anticoagulants is bleeding, and older adults may be more susceptible to bleeding events, which can be severe or even life-threatening.

B. Gender

Women are more likely to experience ADRs than men, possibly due to hormonal differences or differences in drug metabolism. The severity of ADRs may also differ between genders, as women may experience more severe or frequent adverse events with certain medications, such as non-steroidal anti-inflammatory drugs (NSAIDs).

C. Genetic factors

Genetic polymorphisms can affect drug metabolism and disposition, leading to increased or decreased drug efficacy or toxicity. For example, some individuals have genetic variations that affect the metabolism of codeine to its active form, morphine, leading to increased risk of respiratory depression and death.

D. Underlying medical conditions

Patients with pre-existing liver or kidney disease may be more susceptible to drug toxicity, as these organs play a major role in drug metabolism and excretion. Additionally, patients with a compromised immune system, such as those with human immunodeficiency virus (HIV) infection, may be more vulnerable to infections associated with immunosuppressive medications.

E. Patient characteristics, such as body weight and composition

Overweight and obese patients may require higher doses of medications, which can increase the risk of toxicity. Additionally, drug distribution may be altered in patients with abnormal body composition, such as those with high body fat percentage.

8.2.2 Drug factors

When a patient experiences an adverse drug reaction (ADR), the severity and seriousness of the reaction can vary widely depending on various drug-related factors. These factors play a critical role in the determination of the overall risk associated with a drug, as well as the appropriateness of its use in certain patient populations. In this section, we will discuss some of the key drug-related factors that can influence ADR severity and seriousness.

Pharmacological Properties: The pharmacological properties of a drug can significantly impact the severity and seriousness of an ADR. Certain drug classes, such as chemotherapeutic agents and immunosuppressants, are known to have a higher risk of severe ADRs. Other factors that can influence the severity of ADRs include the drug's potency, dose, duration of therapy, and route of administration. For example, drugs that are administered via injection or inhalation may have a more rapid onset of action, which can increase the risk of severe ADRs.

Pharmacokinetics: The pharmacokinetic properties of a drug, such as its absorption, distribution, metabolism, and elimination, can also impact the severity and seriousness of an ADR. For example, drugs that are metabolized by the liver may have a higher risk of toxicity in patients with hepatic impairment. Similarly, drugs that are eliminated by the kidneys may have a higher risk of toxicity in patients with renal impairment.

Drug Interactions: Drug-drug interactions can significantly impact the severity and seriousness of ADRs. Some drugs can interact with other medications, altering their pharmacokinetic and pharmacodynamic properties, and potentially increasing the risk of adverse events. For example, combining certain antidepressants with monoamine oxidase inhibitors (MAOIs) can result in serotonin syndrome, a potentially life-threatening condition characterized by fever, muscle rigidity, and seizures.

Formulation and Manufacturing: The formulation and manufacturing process of a drug can also influence the severity and seriousness of ADRs. Certain excipients used in drug formulations, such as preservatives and dyes, can cause allergic reactions in susceptible patients. Similarly, manufacturing defects or contamination can result in unexpected adverse events.

Genetic Factors: Genetic factors can also play a role in the severity and seriousness of ADRs. Genetic variations in drug-metabolizing enzymes and transporters can impact the pharmacokinetics and pharmacodynamics of drugs, leading to increased toxicity or decreased efficacy. For example, patients with a genetic variation in the CYP2D6 gene may be poor metabolizers of codeine, resulting in reduced analgesic efficacy and an increased risk of respiratory depression.

8.2.3 Disease factors

Disease Severity: The severity of a disease can affect the severity and seriousness of ADRs. Patients with severe underlying disease may be more susceptible to adverse effects due to decreased organ function or altered pharmacokinetics. For example, patients with severe liver disease may be at an increased risk of developing hepatotoxicity from certain drugs.

Disease Progression: The progression of a disease can also influence ADR severity and seriousness. As a disease progresses, it can affect various organs and systems, leading to changes in drug metabolism and elimination. This can result in an increased risk of adverse effects. For example, in cancer patients undergoing chemotherapy, the severity and seriousness of ADRs can increase as the disease progresses and the patient becomes more immunocompromised.

Concomitant Medications: Patients with certain diseases may require multiple medications, which can increase the risk of drug interactions and ADRs. For example, patients with HIV/AIDS may require antiretroviral therapy along with medications to manage opportunistic infections. The concomitant use of multiple medications can increase the risk of drug interactions and ADRs.

Genetic Factors: Some diseases are associated with genetic variations that can affect drug metabolism and response, leading to an increased risk of ADRs. For example, patients with genetic variations in the TPMT gene may be at an increased risk of developing myelosuppression from thiopurine drugs.

Age: Certain diseases are more prevalent in specific age groups, and the age of the patient can also influence ADR severity and seriousness. For example, elderly patients with Parkinson's disease may be at an increased risk of developing delirium from anticholinergic medications due to age-related changes in pharmacokinetics and pharmacodynamics.

Examples of Disease Factors Influencing ADR Severity and Seriousness:

Inflammatory Bowel Disease (IBD): Patients with IBD, including Crohn's disease and ulcerative colitis, may require immunosuppressive medications, which can increase the risk of infections and other ADRs. The severity of the disease can also affect the risk of ADRs. For example, patients with severe IBD may require biologic therapies, which can increase the risk of infusion reactions and other serious ADRs.

Cancer: Patients undergoing cancer treatment may experience a range of ADRs, including chemotherapy-induced nausea and vomiting, myelosuppression, and peripheral neuropathy. The severity and seriousness of these ADRs can vary depending on the type and stage of cancer, as well as the type of chemotherapy and radiation therapy used.

Cardiovascular Disease: Patients with cardiovascular disease may require multiple medications, including anticoagulants, antiplatelet agents, and lipid-lowering drugs. The concomitant use of these medications can increase the risk of drug interactions and ADRs. Additionally, patients with severe heart failure may be at an increased risk of developing renal impairment from certain medications due to decreased renal perfusion.

8.2.4 Other factors

Gender: Gender differences may play a role in the severity and seriousness of ADRs. For example, women may be more susceptible to certain ADRs due to hormonal differences. Men may be more likely to experience adverse effects related to sexual function.

Genetic factors: Genetic factors can impact how a patient responds to a drug and can influence the severity and seriousness of an ADR. For example, genetic testing can identify patients who are at increased risk for certain ADRs such as drug-induced liver injury.

Concurrent diseases or conditions: Patients with underlying medical conditions may be more susceptible to ADRs or may experience more severe ADRs. For example, patients with renal impairment may be at increased risk for drug accumulation and toxicity.

Duration of therapy: The length of time a patient has been taking a drug can influence the severity and seriousness of an ADR. Longer exposure to a drug can increase the likelihood of ADRs and can also increase the severity of the ADR.

Dose and route of administration: The dose and route of administration of a drug can influence the severity and seriousness of an ADR. Higher doses or more invasive routes of administration (e.g., intravenous vs oral) can increase the likelihood of ADRs.

Quality of healthcare: The quality of healthcare can influence the severity and seriousness of ADRs. Patients who receive suboptimal care, including inadequate monitoring or inappropriate drug selection, may be more susceptible to ADRs.

Patient adherence: Patient adherence to medication regimens can impact the severity and seriousness of ADRs. Patients who do not follow prescribed medication regimens may be at increased risk for ADRs.

8.3 Methods for Assessing ADR Severity and Seriousness

Assessing the severity and seriousness of an Adverse Drug Reaction (ADR) is critical for understanding the impact of a medication on a patient's health. There are various methods for evaluating the severity and seriousness of ADRs.

1. Common Scales and Criteria

A.Common Terminology Criteria for Adverse Events (CTCAE):

The Common Terminology Criteria for Adverse Events (CTCAE) is a widely used tool for assessing the severity and seriousness of adverse drug reactions (ADRs). CTCAE was developed by the National Cancer Institute (NCI) to standardize the classification of adverse events (AEs) associated with cancer treatments. However, it has been widely adopted in other areas of medicine as well, including clinical trials and post-marketing surveillance of drugs.

The CTCAE is a set of criteria that classifies the severity of AEs on a scale of 1 to 5, with 1 being the mildest and 5 being the most severe. The criteria also take into account the impact of the AE on the patient's daily activities and the need for medical intervention. The severity scale is as follows:

Grade 1: Mild AE, usually not requiring treatment

Grade 2: Moderate AE, requiring minimal or local treatment

Grade 3: Severe AE, requiring systemic treatment or hospitalization

Grade 4: Life-threatening AE, requiring urgent intervention

Grade 5: Fatal AE

The CTCAE also includes criteria for assessing the seriousness of AEs, which are defined as any event that results in death, hospitalization or prolongation of existing hospitalization, persistent or significant disability or incapacity, or a congenital anomaly or birth defect. Serious AEs are categorized as either "unanticipated" or "anticipated" based on whether or not they were expected to occur based on the drug's known safety profile.

The CTCAE has several advantages as a tool for assessing ADR severity and seriousness. Firstly, it provides a standardized approach to categorizing AEs, which improves consistency and comparability across different studies and settings. This is particularly important in clinical trials, where ADRs are a primary endpoint of interest. Secondly, the CTCAE takes into account the impact of AEs on the patient's daily activities and need for medical intervention, which helps clinicians prioritize and manage AEs in a more efficient manner. Finally, the CTCAE is regularly updated to reflect changes in drug safety knowledge, which ensures that it remains a relevant and reliable tool for assessing ADR severity and seriousness over time.

However, the CTCAE also has some limitations. One limitation is that it may not capture all aspects of ADR severity and seriousness, particularly for drugs with unique or rare AEs that may not be fully captured by the standard criteria. Another limitation is that the CTCAE may not account for patient-specific factors that may impact the severity and seriousness of ADRs, such as age, gender, and comorbidities. Therefore, it is important for clinicians to consider these factors when interpreting CTCAE scores and making treatment decisions.

CTCAE is a valuable tool for assessing the severity and seriousness of ADRs in clinical practice and research. Its standardized approach improves consistency and comparability, and its regular updates ensure that it remains relevant and reliable over time. However, clinicians should be aware of its limitations and supplement it with additional information as needed to make informed treatment decisions

B. Hartwig Severity Assessment Scale

The Hartwig Severity Assessment Scale is a widely used tool for assessing the severity of adverse drug reactions (ADRs). The scale was developed by Hartwig et al. in 1992 and is based on a 10-point scale, with higher scores indicating more severe ADRs.

The Hartwig Severity Assessment Scale considers the following factors in assessing the severity of an ADR:

The nature of the ADR: Some ADRs are more severe than others due to their clinical consequences, such as life-threatening or disabling events.

The dose of the drug: Higher doses of a drug may lead to more severe ADRs.

The time course of the ADR: ADRs that occur soon after drug initiation or with short-term use are generally considered more severe than those that occur after longer-term use.

The predictability of the ADR: ADRs that are more predictable based on the drug's pharmacological properties or previous reports are generally considered less severe.

Each ADR is assigned a score between 0 and 9 based on the severity of the reaction, with higher scores indicating more severe reactions. The scores are as follows: 0 - no symptoms 1 - mild symptoms 2 - moderate symptoms 3 - severe symptoms requiring hospitalization 4 - life-threatening symptoms requiring intensive care 5 - fatal outcome 6 - disability or permanent damage 7 - congenital anomaly or birth defect 8 - required intervention to prevent permanent impairment or damage 9 - other serious consequences.

The Hartwig Severity Assessment Scale has been used in many studies and clinical trials to assess the severity of ADRs. For example, a study published in the Journal of Clinical Pharmacy and Therapeutics in 2012 used the Hartwig Severity Assessment Scale to assess the severity of ADRs in elderly patients taking multiple medications. The study found that the scale was a reliable tool for assessing the severity of ADRs and could be used to identify high-risk patients who may benefit from medication review and monitoring.

Another study published in the Journal of Pharmacovigilance in 2016 used the Hartwig Severity Assessment Scale to assess the severity of ADRs associated with the use of nonsteroidal anti-inflammatory drugs (NSAIDs). The study found that the majority of ADRs were mild or moderate in severity, but there were some cases of severe ADRs requiring hospitalization.

Hartwig Severity Assessment Scale is a useful tool for assessing the severity of ADRs and has been validated in many studies. Its use can help healthcare professionals identify and prioritize the management of more severe ADRs, and may help in the development of interventions to reduce the incidence and severity of ADRs.

C. Schumock and Thornton Criteria

The Schumock and Thornton criteria is a widely used method for assessing the severity and seriousness of adverse drug reactions (ADRs). It was first introduced in 1992 and has since been modified and updated to reflect changes in medical practice and drug therapy.

The Schumock and Thornton criteria categorize ADRs based on their severity and seriousness. Severity refers to the intensity of the ADR, while seriousness refers to the potential consequences of the ADR, such as hospitalization, disability, or death. The criteria use a five-point scale to assess severity, ranging from mild to fatal, and a three-point scale to assess seriousness, ranging from non-serious to life-threatening.

The Schumock and Thornton criteria take into account various factors that may influence the severity and seriousness of an ADR, such as the patient's age and medical history, the dose and duration of the drug therapy, and the presence of other medications or medical conditions.

Some examples of how the Schumock and Thornton criteria may be applied in practice include:

- A patient who experiences a mild skin rash after starting a new medication would be classified as having a mild ADR of non-serious severity.
- A patient who experiences severe nausea and vomiting after taking a high dose of a chemotherapy drug would be classified as having a severe ADR of serious severity.
- A patient who experiences a life-threatening anaphylactic reaction after receiving a contrast agent during a medical imaging procedure would be classified as having a life-threatening ADR of critical severity.

The Schumock and Thornton criteria have been used in numerous studies and clinical trials to assess the severity and seriousness of ADRs. They are also commonly used by regulatory agencies and healthcare providers to monitor and report ADRs, as well as to guide treatment decisions and risk management strategies.

However, like any assessment method, the Schumock and Thornton criteria have limitations and may not always capture the full complexity of ADRs. They also rely on subjective judgments and may be influenced by individual biases and variations in clinical practice. Therefore, it is important to use multiple assessment methods and to consider the context and individual characteristics of each ADR when determining its severity and seriousness.

2. The French Society of Pharmacology and Therapeutics (SFPT) Scale

The French Society of Pharmacology and Therapeutics (SFPT) Scale is a method for assessing the severity of adverse drug reactions (ADRs) based on the clinical symptoms and laboratory data associated with the ADR. The SFPT scale consists of five grades of severity ranging from 0 to 4:

Grade 0: no symptoms

Grade 1: mild symptoms that do not require any specific treatment

Grade 2: moderate symptoms that require specific treatment but are not life-threatening

Grade 3: severe symptoms that are life-threatening or require hospitalization

Grade 4: fatal outcome

The SFPT scale has been widely used in France and other European countries for the assessment of ADR severity. It is considered to be a useful tool for the early detection and management of ADRs, as well as for monitoring the safety of drugs in clinical practice.

For example, a study conducted in a French hospital found that the SFPT scale was effective in identifying severe ADRs in patients admitted to the hospital. The study also found that the SFPT scale was useful for assessing the severity of ADRs and for guiding treatment decisions in patients with multiple ADRs.

However, like other severity assessment scales, the SFPT scale has some limitations. One limitation is that it relies heavily on subjective clinical judgment, which can lead to variability in the severity grading between different healthcare professionals. Another limitation is that the scale does not take into account the underlying medical conditions of the patient, which can affect the severity of the ADR. Despite these limitations, the SFPT scale remains a valuable tool for the assessment of ADR severity and for improving patient safety in clinical practice.

3. Other Methods for Assessing ADR Severity and Seriousness

Expert Judgment: Expert judgment involves the use of trained professionals to evaluate the severity and seriousness of an ADR based on their knowledge and experience in the field. This method is commonly used when there is a lack of standardized criteria or scales to assess ADR severity and seriousness. Experts can take into account various factors such as the patient's medical history, the drug's mechanism of action, and the nature of the adverse event to make their judgment.

Patient-Reported Outcomes: Patient-reported outcomes (PROs) are measures of health or quality of life directly reported by the patient. In the context of ADR severity and seriousness assessment, PROs can provide valuable information about the impact of the adverse event on the patient's life. This includes the level of pain, discomfort, and disability caused by the ADR, as well as the effect on the patient's daily activities, work, and social life. PROs can be assessed through various methods, such as questionnaires, interviews, and diaries.

While expert judgment and PROs are not standardized methods for assessing ADR severity and seriousness, they can provide valuable information in certain situations. For example, expert judgment may be useful when dealing with rare or novel adverse events, where standardized scales are not available. PROs can be particularly useful in assessing the impact of ADRs on the patient's quality of life, which may not always be captured by objective measures of severity and seriousness.

While standardized scales and criteria are important tools for assessing ADR severity and seriousness, it is important to also consider other methods, such as expert judgment and PROs, to provide a more comprehensive understanding of the impact of ADRs on patients.

8.4 Challenges

Adverse drug reactions (ADRs) are a significant public health concern and can result in increased morbidity, mortality, and healthcare costs. The severity and seriousness of ADRs can vary widely and depend on a variety of factors. Accurate and standardized assessment of ADR severity and seriousness is crucial for effective clinical management and pharmacovigilance. However, there are several challenges associated with the assessment of ADR severity and seriousness.

A. Subjectivity of Assessment: One of the primary challenges in ADR severity and seriousness assessment is the subjectivity of the assessment process. ADR assessment typically involves subjective judgments by healthcare professionals, and there may be significant variation in the assessments made by different clinicians. This subjectivity can lead to inconsistent and unreliable assessments of ADR severity and seriousness, which can impede effective pharmacovigilance.

B. Lack of Standardization: Another challenge in ADR severity and seriousness assessment is the lack of standardization in assessment methods. There are numerous scales and criteria available for assessing ADR severity and seriousness, and healthcare professionals may use different methods or criteria, leading to inconsistent and unreliable assessments. This lack of standardization makes it challenging to compare ADR severity and seriousness assessments across studies or healthcare settings.

C. Limited Information: A third challenge in ADR severity and seriousness assessment is the limited information available to healthcare professionals. In some cases, ADRs may be rare or difficult to detect, and there may be limited information available on the severity and seriousness of the ADR. This limited information can make it challenging for healthcare professionals to accurately assess the severity and seriousness of ADRs.

8.5 Future Directions

A. Improved Standardization and Guidelines: One key area for future development in ADR severity and seriousness assessment is the development of standardized assessment methods and guidelines. The standardization of assessment methods and criteria can improve the reliability and consistency of ADR severity and seriousness assessments across different healthcare settings and studies.

B. Use of New Technologies: Another area for future development is the use of new technologies, such as machine learning and artificial intelligence, to improve ADR severity and seriousness assessment. These technologies can help to automate the assessment process and reduce the subjectivity of assessments.

C. Greater Patient Involvement: Another area for future development is greater patient involvement in ADR severity and seriousness assessment. Patient-reported outcomes can provide valuable information on the severity and seriousness of ADRs, and involving patients in the assessment process can improve the accuracy and reliability of assessments.

D. Increased Collaboration between Stakeholders: Finally, increased collaboration between stakeholders, including healthcare professionals, patients, regulatory agencies, and pharmaceutical companies, can help to improve ADR severity and seriousness assessment. Collaboration can improve the quality and completeness of data on ADRs, which can improve the accuracy and reliability of assessments.

IX
Predictability and Preventability

9.1 Introduction

Predictability and preventability assessment is a critical component of pharmacovigilance, which involves the assessment of the likelihood of an adverse drug reaction (ADR) occurring and the extent to which it can be prevented. Predictability refers to the ability to anticipate the occurrence of an ADR, based on the known pharmacological properties of the drug and the patient's characteristics. Preventability refers to the extent to which an ADR can be avoided or minimized through appropriate measures, such as dose adjustment, drug discontinuation, or supportive care.

9.2 Importance of predictability and preventability assessment in pharmacovigilance

The assessment of predictability and preventability is essential in pharmacovigilance for several reasons. First, it allows for the early detection of potential safety concerns, which can lead to timely regulatory action to protect public health. For example, the prediction of liver toxicity associated with the use of troglitazone led to its withdrawal from the market.

Second, it enables the implementation of risk management strategies to minimize the occurrence of ADRs. This can involve identifying patient populations at higher risk of developing ADRs and implementing targeted monitoring and prevention strategies. For example, individuals with a history of allergic reactions to drugs may be monitored more closely for signs of hypersensitivity when prescribed new medications.

Third, it can inform the development of new drugs and the improvement of existing ones, by providing insights into the underlying mechanisms of ADRs and the factors that contribute to their occurrence and preventability. This can lead to the development of safer drugs with fewer side effects and better therapeutic outcomes.

Examples of the importance of predictability and preventability assessment in pharmacovigilance include the withdrawal of cerivastatin, a cholesterol-lowering drug, due to a high risk of fatal rhabdomyolysis, and the development of the REMS (Risk Evaluation and Mitigation Strategy) program for certain drugs associated with a high risk of serious ADRs, such as isotretinoin, to ensure their safe use.

Furthermore, the assessment of predictability and preventability is essential in the context of personalized medicine, where patient-specific factors, such as genetic variations, may influence the occurrence and preventability of ADRs. The identification of genetic markers associated with drug-induced ADRs can help predict the likelihood of an ADR occurring and enable the development of personalized prevention and treatment strategies.

The assessment of predictability and preventability is a critical component of pharmacovigilance, which can lead to the early detection of potential safety concerns, the implementation of risk management strategies, and the development of safer drugs with better therapeutic outcomes. It is essential that regulatory bodies, healthcare professionals, and patients are aware of the importance of predictability and preventability assessment and work together to ensure its effective implementation in clinical practice.

9.3 Predictability Assessment

Definition and factors affecting predictability

In pharmacovigilance, predictability assessment refers to the likelihood that a particular adverse drug reaction (ADR) will occur in a patient based on the drug's pharmacological properties and the patient's individual characteristics. This assessment is important for identifying and managing the risks associated with drug therapy.

Several factors can affect predictability, including the drug's pharmacological properties, such as its mechanism of action, pharmacokinetics, and pharmacodynamics. The patient's individual characteristics, such as age, sex, underlying medical conditions, and concomitant medications, can also affect predictability. Other factors, such as dosing regimen, duration of therapy, and route of administration, can also influence predictability.

For example, certain drugs, such as chemotherapy agents, have a higher likelihood of causing ADRs due to their mechanism of action and toxicity. Similarly, certain patient populations, such as the elderly or those with multiple comorbidities, may be more susceptible to ADRs due to changes in pharmacokinetics and pharmacodynamics. Additionally, concomitant use of other medications can increase the risk of ADRs through drug-drug interactions.

Methods for predictability assessment

A. In vitro and in vivo assays

In vitro and in vivo assays are methods used for predictability assessment in pharmacovigilance. In vitro assays involve testing a drug in a laboratory setting using cells or tissues to determine its effects on biological pathways or specific targets. These assays can help identify potential adverse effects of a drug, such as toxicity or mutagenicity, before it is tested in animals or humans. In vitro assays can also help in identifying drug-drug interactions and evaluating the potential for idiosyncratic drug reactions.

In vivo assays involve testing a drug in a live animal model to evaluate its pharmacological effects and potential toxicity. These assays can provide valuable information on the pharmacokinetics and pharmacodynamics of a drug, as well as its potential for toxicity and efficacy. In vivo assays can also be used to identify specific organ toxicities or target-organ effects, which can aid in the prediction of ADRs in humans.

However, in vitro and in vivo assays have limitations, such as the potential for false positive or false negative results due to differences in animal physiology or extrapolation from animal to human data. These limitations can be addressed by using multiple assays and models to improve predictability.

B. Pharmacogenetic Testing

Pharmacogenetic testing is another method used for predictability assessment in pharmacovigilance. This involves analyzing a patient's genetic makeup to predict their response to a drug and identify potential ADRs. Pharmacogenetic testing can also aid in dose optimization and drug selection, which can reduce the risk of ADRs.

For example, the drug abacavir, used for the treatment of HIV, is associated with a high risk of hypersensitivity reactions in patients with a specific genetic variant. Pharmacogenetic testing can help identify patients at risk for this reaction and avoid the use of this drug in these individuals.

However, pharmacogenetic testing has limitations, such as the need for specialized equipment and expertise, as well as the potential for ethical and legal concerns related to genetic testing.

C. Machine Learning

Machine learning is an emerging method used for predictability assessment in pharmacovigilance. This involves using artificial intelligence algorithms to analyze large datasets of ADRs and identify patterns and associations between drugs and ADRs. Machine learning can also aid in signal detection and drug safety surveillance.

For example, a study conducted by the FDA used machine learning algorithms to identify a potential association between the drug fluoxetine and abnormal bleeding events. This led to a warning label update for the drug.

However, machine learning also has limitations, such as the potential for bias and the need for high-quality data. These limitations can be addressed by using multiple algorithms and datasets to improve accuracy and reduce bias.

D. Animal Models :

Animal models are also used to assess the predictability of ADRs. Preclinical animal studies are conducted before a drug is tested in humans to evaluate the safety and efficacy of the drug. Animal models can provide valuable information on potential ADRs that may occur in humans. Animal studies can identify ADRs that may not have been detected in in vitro or in silico models.

Animal models can be used to assess both the dose-response relationship and the temporal relationship between drug exposure and the onset of ADRs. Dose-response studies can provide information on the minimum effective dose and the dose at which toxicity occurs. Temporal relationship studies can provide information on the onset and duration of ADRs.

However, it is important to note that animal models may not accurately reflect the response of humans to a drug. Animals may have different physiological responses to drugs, and the dose of the drug required to produce an effect may be different in animals than in humans. Therefore, caution should be exercised when interpreting animal data, and animal studies should be complemented with human studies to validate the findings.

One example of the use of animal models in predictability assessment is the case of thalidomide. Thalidomide was a drug that was widely prescribed in the 1950s and 1960s to pregnant women for the treatment of morning sickness. However, it was later discovered that thalidomide caused severe birth defects in infants. Animal studies conducted before the approval of thalidomide did not reveal any evidence of teratogenicity. It was later discovered that thalidomide was metabolized differently in humans than in animals, leading to its teratogenic effects in humans. This case highlights the importance of validating animal data with human studies to ensure the predictability of ADRs.

E. Clinical trials and observational studies

Clinical trials and observational studies are also methods used for predictability assessment. Clinical trials are typically designed to test the efficacy of a drug, but they also provide an opportunity to evaluate the safety of a drug. Observational studies, on the other hand, are non-experimental studies that involve the collection of data from existing sources, such as electronic health records or administrative databases.

In clinical trials, adverse events are typically monitored using standardized methods, including questionnaires, physical examinations, and laboratory tests. The results of clinical trials can provide valuable information on the predictability of adverse events associated with a drug. However, it is important to note that clinical trials are typically conducted in a controlled setting and involve a relatively small number of patients, which may limit the generalizability of the results to the broader population.

Observational studies can be useful for assessing the predictability of adverse events associated with a drug in real-world settings. These studies can provide valuable information on the frequency and nature of adverse events associated with a drug, as well as potential risk factors. However, it is important to note that observational studies are subject to several limitations, including the potential for bias and confounding, as well as the lack of control over the study design.

Clinical trials and observational studies can provide valuable information on the predictability of adverse events associated with a drug. However, it is important to use multiple methods for predictability assessment to ensure that the results are robust and reliable.

9.4 Examples of predictability assessment

A. There are numerous examples of predictability assessment in pharmacovigilance. One such example is the case of thalidomide, a drug that was prescribed in the 1950s and 1960s as a sedative and treatment for morning sickness in pregnant women. It was later found to cause severe birth defects in infants, including limb malformations. The predictability assessment in this case involved animal studies and clinical trials that failed to detect the teratogenic effects of the drug. The lack of predictability led to tragic consequences, with an estimated 10,000 infants born with thalidomide-related birth defects.

Another example of predictability assessment involves the drug rosiglitazone, which was used to treat type 2 diabetes. Clinical trials showed that the drug increased the risk of cardiovascular events, and the drug was subsequently withdrawn from the market. The predictability assessment in this case involved the use of clinical trials to detect the potential ADRs associated with the drug.

A more recent example is the case of hydroxychloroquine, a drug that was initially thought to be a potential treatment for COVID-19. However, clinical trials and observational studies failed to demonstrate any significant benefit, and the drug was ultimately not recommended for use in treating COVID-19. The predictability assessment in this case involved the use of clinical trials and observational studies to evaluate the safety and efficacy of the drug in treating COVID-19.

These examples highlight the importance of predictability assessment in pharmacovigilance and the need for robust and reliable methods for detecting potential ADRs.

B. Stevens-Johnson Syndrome and Carbamazepine

Stevens-Johnson Syndrome (SJS) is a rare, but potentially life-threatening, hypersensitivity reaction that is characterized by skin rash, fever, and mucosal lesions. SJS is most commonly triggered by exposure to certain drugs, including carbamazepine, an antiepileptic medication that is also used to treat neuropathic pain and mood disorders.

Carbamazepine-induced SJS has been extensively studied, and predictability assessment has been performed to evaluate the likelihood of SJS occurring in patients taking carbamazepine. In vitro assays have shown that carbamazepine can stimulate T-cell activation and proliferation, which can lead to a hypersensitivity reaction in susceptible individuals. Animal models have also been used to evaluate the potential for carbamazepine-induced SJS, with results suggesting that the severity of the reaction is dose-dependent.

Clinical trials and observational studies have also been conducted to assess the predictability of carbamazepine-induced SJS in humans. A study published in the New England Journal of Medicine found that patients with a particular genetic marker, HLA-B*1502, were at an increased risk of developing SJS when taking carbamazepine. The study was conducted in a Han Chinese population and led to a recommendation to screen for the genetic marker in patients of Han Chinese ancestry before prescribing carbamazepine.

Thus, the predictability assessment of carbamazepine-induced SJS has led to improved patient safety through genetic screening and monitoring for early signs of the condition in patients taking the medication.

C. Drug-induced Liver Injury and Troglitazone

Troglitazone is a thiazolidinedione drug used for the treatment of type 2 diabetes. However, it was withdrawn from the market in 2000 due to cases of drug-induced liver injury (DILI). DILI is a serious adverse drug reaction that can result in liver failure and even death. The withdrawal of troglitazone led to an increased focus on predicting and preventing DILI.

Several studies have since been conducted to assess the predictability of DILI. One study used data from clinical trials to identify risk factors for DILI associated with troglitazone. The study found that age, female gender, and elevated liver enzymes at baseline were significant risk factors for DILI. This information could be used to identify patients who are at higher risk of developing DILI and to monitor them closely for signs of liver injury.

Another study used in vitro assays to predict the potential for DILI associated with new drug candidates. The study found that a high percentage of compounds that were identified as potential DILI candidates in vitro also exhibited DILI in clinical trials. This suggests that in vitro assays can be a useful tool for predicting DILI.

Observational studies have also been used to assess the predictability of DILI. One study used data from a large observational study to identify risk factors for DILI associated with several drugs, including troglitazone. The study found that older age, female gender, and concurrent use of other drugs were significant risk factors for DILI.

9.5 Preventability Assessment

A. Definition and factors affecting preventability

Preventability assessment is the evaluation of the likelihood that an adverse drug reaction (ADR) could have been avoided with appropriate measures. It involves assessing the extent to which ADRs could have been prevented by actions such as avoiding the drug, reducing the dose, or monitoring the patient more closely. Preventability assessment is an essential component of pharmacovigilance as it provides insights into how ADRs can be avoided or minimized.

Several factors can affect the preventability of ADRs. These include patient-related factors such as age, sex, genetics, and comorbidities, as well as drug-related factors such as dose, duration of treatment, and drug interactions. Healthcare system-related factors such as access to healthcare, medication errors, and quality of care can also influence preventability.

B. Methods for preventability assessment

Various methods are used for preventability assessment, including expert panels, case-by-case reviews, and computer algorithms. Expert panels typically consist of clinicians, pharmacists, and other healthcare professionals who review ADR cases to determine their preventability. They may use predefined criteria, such as the Schumock and Thornton criteria, to assess preventability.

Case-by-case reviews involve analyzing individual ADR cases to determine if they were preventable. This method is time-consuming and may not be practical for large datasets.

Computer algorithms can also be used for preventability assessment. These algorithms use predefined criteria and data from electronic health records (EHRs) to assess the preventability of ADRs automatically. While this method is faster than manual review, it may not be as accurate as expert panels or case-by-case reviews.

Prospective and retrospective studies

Prospective and retrospective studies are two types of observational studies used in preventability assessment. In prospective studies, participants are enrolled before exposure to a drug or other intervention, and they are followed over time to determine if any adverse events occur. Retrospective studies, on the other hand, involve looking back at existing data, such as medical records or insurance claims, to identify cases of adverse events that occurred in the past.

Prospective studies can be further divided into randomized controlled trials (RCTs) and non-randomized studies. RCTs are considered the gold standard in clinical research because they involve randomly assigning participants to a treatment group or control group, which helps minimize the effects of confounding variables. Non-randomized studies, such as cohort studies and case-control studies, are also used in prospective preventability assessment.

Retrospective studies are often used when it is not feasible or ethical to conduct a prospective study, such as when the adverse event is rare or when the intervention has already been widely used. They can also be used to supplement the results of prospective studies or to generate hypotheses for future studies.

Both prospective and retrospective studies have their strengths and weaknesses. Prospective studies can provide more reliable data because they involve following participants over time, but they can be costly and time-consuming. Retrospective studies are often quicker and less expensive, but they may be subject to bias or confounding variables.

In preventability assessment, both prospective and retrospective studies can be used to identify risk factors for adverse events and to determine if these events could have been prevented. For example, a prospective study may be conducted to evaluate the preventability of adverse events associated with a new drug, while a retrospective study may be used to assess the preventability of adverse events associated with a widely used drug that has been on the market for several years. By combining the results of these studies, researchers can gain a more comprehensive understanding of the preventability of adverse events and develop strategies to minimize the risk of these events occurring in the future.

Root cause analysis (RCA) is a method used in healthcare to identify the underlying causes of an adverse event or error. RCA is a systematic approach that involves a multidisciplinary team, usually consisting of healthcare professionals, risk managers, and patient safety experts, who work together to identify the root cause(s) of an adverse event.

The RCA process involves several steps, including data collection and analysis, identification of the contributing factors, and development of corrective and preventive actions to address the root cause(s) of the adverse event. RCA is often conducted retrospectively, after an adverse event has occurred, but it can also be conducted prospectively to identify potential risks before they result in an adverse event.

RCA is an important tool in preventability assessment because it allows healthcare organizations to identify areas for improvement and implement strategies to prevent future adverse events. By addressing the root cause(s) of an adverse event, healthcare organizations can reduce the likelihood of similar events occurring in the future.

One example of the use of RCA in preventability assessment is the analysis of medication errors in a hospital setting. A multidisciplinary team may review the factors that contributed to medication errors, such as inadequate training of staff, poor communication, or unclear labeling of medications. Based on the findings, the team may develop and implement strategies to address these issues, such as providing additional training to staff, improving communication protocols, or redesigning medication labeling.

Overall, RCA is a valuable method for preventability assessment because it allows healthcare organizations to identify and address the underlying causes of adverse events, ultimately leading to improved patient safety and outcomes.

Expert panel review

Expert panel review is a method used to assess the preventability of an adverse drug reaction (ADR) by convening a group of experts in the relevant fields to evaluate the case. This method involves a group of experts, typically including clinicians, pharmacologists, and other relevant specialists, who review the case in question and discuss the factors that may have contributed to the ADR.

The expert panel review process typically involves a structured approach to evaluating the case, including a review of the patient's medical history, medications, and any other relevant information. The panel may also review published literature on the drug in question and similar cases of ADRs to gain a broader perspective.

The expert panel may use a scoring system to assess the preventability of the ADR, assigning scores to various factors that may have contributed to the event. These factors may include the severity of the ADR, the patient's underlying medical condition, the dose and duration of the medication, and any other relevant factors.

Expert panel review can provide valuable insights into the preventability of ADRs and can help to identify areas for improvement in medication safety. However, it is important to ensure that the panel members are appropriately qualified and have relevant expertise in the area under review to ensure accurate and reliable assessments.

Overall, expert panel review is a useful method for preventability assessment in pharmacovigilance and can provide valuable insights into the underlying causes of ADRs.

9.6 Examples of preventability assessment

A. One example of preventability assessment is the use of medication reconciliation in hospitals to prevent medication errors. Medication reconciliation is a process that involves comparing a patient's current medications with those ordered by healthcare providers to identify any discrepancies and prevent errors. A study conducted in a hospital in the United States found that implementing medication reconciliation reduced the number of preventable adverse drug events by 66%.

Another example is the implementation of a computerized physician order entry (CPOE) system to prevent medication errors. CPOE systems allow healthcare providers to enter medication orders electronically, which are then checked for potential errors, such as incorrect dosages or drug interactions. A study conducted in a hospital in Australia found that implementing a CPOE system reduced the number of medication errors by 60%.

Furthermore, the use of patient education programs to prevent medication errors is another example of preventability assessment. Patient education programs provide information to patients about their medications, including dosages, potential side effects, and instructions for use. A study conducted in a hospital in the United States found that implementing a patient education program reduced medication errors by 40%.

In all these examples, preventability assessment plays a crucial role in identifying potential areas for improvement in medication safety and implementing interventions to prevent future errors and adverse events.

B. Adverse drug reactions associated with NSAIDs

Nonsteroidal anti-inflammatory drugs (NSAIDs) are a class of drugs commonly used for the treatment of pain, fever, and inflammation. However, they are also associated with a range of adverse drug reactions (ADRs), including gastrointestinal bleeding, renal toxicity, and cardiovascular events.

A preventability assessment of ADRs associated with NSAIDs was conducted in a study published in the Journal of Clinical Pharmacy and Therapeutics. The study analyzed data from a large US healthcare system and found that 27% of ADRs associated with NSAIDs were preventable. The most common preventable ADRs were gastrointestinal bleeding and renal toxicity, which accounted for 43% and 30% of preventable ADRs, respectively.

The study identified several factors that contributed to preventable ADRs associated with NSAIDs, including inappropriate prescribing, medication errors, and inadequate monitoring of patients. The authors suggested that targeted interventions, such as educational programs for healthcare providers and improved monitoring of patients taking NSAIDs, could help to prevent these ADRs.

Another study published in the Journal of Clinical Gastroenterology conducted a preventability assessment of ADRs associated with the use of non-selective NSAIDs and cyclooxygenase-2 (COX-2) inhibitors. The study found that 66% of ADRs associated with non-selective NSAIDs and 64% of ADRs associated with COX-2 inhibitors were preventable. The most common preventable ADRs were gastrointestinal bleeding and renal toxicity.

The study identified several factors that contributed to preventable ADRs associated with NSAIDs, including inappropriate dosing, drug interactions, and inadequate monitoring of patients. The authors suggested that targeted interventions, such as improved prescribing practices and patient monitoring, could help to prevent these ADRs.

9.7 Preventable ADRs in hospitalized patients

Preventability assessment has also been used to evaluate adverse drug reactions (ADRs) in hospitalized patients. Several studies have been conducted to identify preventable ADRs and determine the factors contributing to their occurrence.

One study conducted in the United States evaluated preventable ADRs in a large tertiary care hospital. The study found that 27% of ADRs were preventable and that medication errors and inadequate patient monitoring were the main factors contributing to preventable ADRs. Another study conducted in a Brazilian hospital found that 50% of ADRs were preventable, with medication errors and prescribing inappropriate medications being the main contributing factors.

In another study, researchers in the United Kingdom conducted a systematic review of preventable ADRs in hospitalized patients. The study found that preventable ADRs were common, and that medication errors, prescribing inappropriate medications, and inadequate patient monitoring were the main contributing factors. The study also found that preventable ADRs were associated with longer hospital stays, increased healthcare costs, and higher mortality rates.

These studies highlight the importance of preventability assessment in identifying and addressing preventable ADRs in hospitalized patients. By identifying the factors contributing to preventable ADRs, healthcare professionals can take steps to reduce the occurrence of these ADRs and improve patient safety.

Examples of preventability assessment

Several studies have been conducted to assess the preventability of ADRs in different patient populations and settings. For example, a study of preventable ADRs in elderly patients found that most were preventable, with drug-related factors such as inappropriate prescribing and dosing being the most common reasons for preventability. Another study of preventable ADRs in hospitalized patients found that preventable ADRs were associated with longer hospital stays and higher healthcare costs.

X
Management of Adverse reactions

10.1 Introduction

Adverse drug reactions (ADRs) refer to unintended and harmful responses to a medication, which can occur at any dose or duration of treatment. They can range from mild symptoms, such as a rash or nausea, to severe reactions, including liver damage or life-threatening allergic reactions. ADRs can have a significant impact on patients' health outcomes, leading to prolonged hospital stays, additional medical costs, and even death. As such, managing ADRs is a critical aspect of patient safety and drug therapy.

Effective management of ADRs requires a comprehensive approach, including prevention, detection, evaluation, and treatment. Prevention of ADRs involves careful selection of medications based on a patient's clinical condition, medical history, and potential risk factors for adverse reactions. It also involves educating patients about the potential risks and benefits of their medications, and monitoring for potential ADRs during treatment.

Detection and evaluation of ADRs involve systematic monitoring and documentation of adverse events associated with drug therapy. This can be done through patient self-reporting, healthcare provider reporting, and laboratory monitoring. The evaluation of ADRs involves assessing the severity and potential causality of the reaction, which can help inform treatment decisions.

Treatment of ADRs can vary depending on the severity and type of reaction. Mild to moderate reactions may require symptomatic treatment, such as the use of antihistamines for a rash or antiemetics for nausea. More severe reactions may require discontinuation of the medication and the use of specific antidotes or supportive care. In some cases, rechallenge with the medication may be necessary to confirm the diagnosis and inform future treatment decisions.

Managing ADRs is a critical aspect of patient safety and drug therapy. Effective management involves a comprehensive approach, including prevention, detection, evaluation, and treatment. Healthcare providers must be vigilant in monitoring for potential ADRs, educating patients about the risks and benefits of their medications, and selecting medications based on a patient's clinical condition and potential risk factors for adverse reactions. By doing so, patients can receive safe and effective drug therapy, and the incidence and impact of ADRs can be minimized.

10.2 Management of ADRs

Adverse drug reactions (ADRs) are a significant burden on healthcare systems worldwide. Managing ADRs involves a multifaceted approach that requires the involvement of both patients and healthcare professionals. This section will explore the different strategies used to manage ADRs, including patient management and healthcare professional management.

10.2.1 Patient Management

Withdrawal of the drug: The first step in managing an ADR is to identify the offending drug and discontinue its use. The decision to withdraw the drug will depend on the severity of the ADR and the patient's clinical status. In some cases, it may be necessary to switch to an alternative drug to treat the patient's condition.

Symptomatic treatment: Symptomatic treatment is used to manage the clinical manifestations of the ADR. For example, antihistamines can be used to treat allergic reactions, while proton pump inhibitors can be used to treat gastric ulcers.

Supportive care: Patients who experience severe ADRs may require supportive care, such as hospitalization and monitoring of vital signs.

10.2.2 Healthcare Professional Management

Reporting ADRs: Healthcare professionals have a responsibility to report ADRs to the relevant regulatory authorities. Reporting ADRs is essential for identifying new and previously unknown ADRs, and for monitoring the safety of drugs on the market.

Identifying and managing drug interactions: Drug interactions can increase the risk of ADRs. Healthcare professionals should be aware of potential drug interactions and should take steps to minimize the risk of ADRs.

Adjusting medication dosage and frequency: The dosage and frequency of medication may need to be adjusted in patients who experience ADRs. For example, patients who experience renal impairment may require a lower dose of medication.

Providing patient education on medication use: Patient education is an essential component of managing ADRs. Patients should be educated on the risks and benefits of medication use, as well as the signs and symptoms of ADRs. Patients should also be encouraged to report any ADRs to their healthcare provider.

Managing ADRs requires a coordinated approach that involves both patients and healthcare professionals. Patient management strategies include withdrawing the drug, providing symptomatic treatment, and offering supportive care. Healthcare professional management strategies include reporting ADRs, identifying and managing drug interactions, adjusting medication dosage and frequency, and providing patient education on medication use. By working together, patients and healthcare professionals can minimize the impact of ADRs on patient health and wellbeing.

10.2.3 Pharmacological management of ADRs

Pharmacological management of ADRs involves the use of medication to manage or treat the adverse effects caused by a drug. The approach to pharmacological management may vary depending on the specific ADR and its severity. Some commonly used pharmacological interventions for ADRs include:

A. Antidotes

Antidotes are drugs that can reverse the effects of certain medications or toxins. They are often used in cases of drug overdose or poisoning. Examples of antidotes used in the management of ADRs include:

Naloxone for opioid overdose

Flumazenil for benzodiazepine overdose

B. Drug discontinuation

Discontinuing the drug causing the ADR is often the first step in managing ADRs. This may involve stopping the drug entirely or reducing the dosage. In some cases, an alternative medication may be prescribed if the original medication cannot be continued.

C. Reversal agents

Reversal agents are drugs that can reverse the effects of certain medications. They are often used in cases of overdose or when the medication cannot be discontinued. Examples of reversal agents used in the management of ADRs include:

1. Protamine for heparin overdose
2. Vitamin K for warfarin overdose

D. Other pharmacological interventions

Other pharmacological interventions may be used to manage specific ADRs. For example:

Antiemetics such as ondansetron or metoclopramide may be used to manage nausea and vomiting caused by certain medications.

Antihistamines such as diphenhydramine or cetirizine may be used to manage allergic reactions.

In addition to pharmacological management, non-pharmacological interventions such as dietary changes, lifestyle modifications, and physical therapy may also be used in the management of ADRs.

The pharmacological management of ADRs should be tailored to the individual patient and their specific ADR. The risks and benefits of each intervention should be carefully considered, and healthcare professionals should work closely with their patients to develop a management plan that is safe and effective.

10.3 Prevention of ADRs

Adverse drug reactions (ADRs) are a significant cause of morbidity and mortality worldwide. Effective management of ADRs involves not only identifying and treating the symptoms but also taking steps to prevent their occurrence. This can be achieved through drug selection, monitoring, patient education, and healthcare professional education.

One critical aspect of preventing ADRs is drug selection and monitoring. Evidence-based guidelines can assist healthcare professionals in selecting appropriate medications for a given condition. Guidelines can take into account factors such as efficacy, safety, dosing, and potential drug interactions. Regular monitoring for adverse effects is also essential. This includes monitoring for potential drug interactions, monitoring vital signs, and laboratory values, and adjusting medication dosages as needed. For example, in patients receiving anticoagulant therapy, regular monitoring of clotting times can help prevent bleeding events.

Patient education is another critical aspect of preventing ADRs. Patients need to be informed about their medications, including proper dosing, timing, and potential side effects. Proper adherence to medication regimens can help prevent adverse effects from incorrect dosing or missed doses. Patients should also be aware of potential ADRs and instructed to report any new symptoms to their healthcare provider. In one study, patient education and monitoring reduced the incidence of ADRs related to warfarin therapy.

Healthcare professional education is also crucial for preventing ADRs. Healthcare professionals should stay up-to-date with current evidence-based guidelines and practices, as these can change over time as new research becomes available. Training programs should also include instruction on recognizing and reporting ADRs. In one study, the implementation of an educational program for healthcare professionals resulted in a significant increase in the reporting of ADRs.

In addition to these measures, several other strategies can help prevent ADRs. These include the use of computerized physician order entry (CPOE) systems to reduce medication errors, the use of electronic health records (EHRs) to monitor drug interactions and adverse effects, and the implementation of medication reconciliation programs to reduce errors related to transitions of care. For example, one study found that the implementation of a CPOE system resulted in a significant reduction in medication errors and ADRs.

10.4 Recognizing and reporting ADRs

Healthcare professionals play a crucial role in recognizing and reporting adverse drug reactions (ADRs) to pharmacovigilance authorities. Identifying ADRs involves a systematic and structured approach that includes monitoring patient symptoms, laboratory values, and vital signs. Recognizing ADRs is essential because it helps prevent the occurrence of similar events in other patients taking the same drug.

Reporting ADRs is equally important because it helps pharmacovigilance authorities monitor the safety of drugs in real-world settings. In most countries, healthcare professionals are required by law to report serious ADRs to regulatory authorities.

However, underreporting of ADRs remains a significant challenge, with estimates suggesting that less than 10% of all ADRs are reported to pharmacovigilance authorities.

Several factors contribute to underreporting of ADRs, including lack of awareness of the reporting system, uncertainty about the causality of the event, and fear of litigation. To address these issues, healthcare professionals need to be educated on the importance of ADR reporting and the methods for reporting ADRs.

Several initiatives have been implemented to improve ADR reporting rates, including simplifying reporting requirements, providing incentives for reporting, and improving data quality through data mining and signal detection. For example, the European Medicines Agency (EMA) has implemented several initiatives to improve ADR reporting, including the development of a single reporting portal for all EU member states, providing financial incentives for reporting, and implementing data mining and signal detection techniques to improve data quality.

Additionally, healthcare professionals can be encouraged to report ADRs through continuing education programs, which provide information on drug safety and ADR reporting. These programs can be designed to be interactive and case-based, allowing healthcare professionals to practice and reinforce their ADR recognition and reporting skills.

For example, in the United States, the Food and Drug Administration (FDA) requires pharmaceutical companies to provide continuing education programs on drug safety and ADR reporting to healthcare professionals as part of their Risk Evaluation and Mitigation Strategies (REMS) programs. These programs have been shown to increase healthcare professionals' knowledge of drug safety and ADR reporting and improve reporting rates.

Recognizing and reporting ADRs is critical for improving patient safety and preventing the occurrence of similar events in other patients. Healthcare professionals need to be educated on the importance of ADR reporting and provided with the necessary tools and resources to recognize and report ADRs. Initiatives to improve ADR reporting rates and continuing education programs can help achieve this goal.

XI

Basic terminologies used in Pharmacovigilance

11.1 Definition of Pharmacovigilance

Pharmacovigilance (PV) is the science and activities related to the detection, assessment, understanding, and prevention of adverse effects or any other drug-related problems. The goal of PV is to promote the safe and rational use of medicines by collecting, analyzing, and assessing data on adverse drug reactions (ADRs) and other drug-related problems.

11.2 Importance of terminologies in Pharmacovigilance

The use of standardized terminologies is crucial in pharmacovigilance to ensure accurate and consistent communication among healthcare professionals, regulatory authorities, and other stakeholders. Standardized terminologies help in the identification, classification, and reporting of ADRs and other drug-related problems, which, in turn, helps to improve patient safety and promote the rational use of medicines.

11.3 Basic Terminologies Used in Pharmacovigilance

A. Terminologies of adverse medication related events

A. Adverse drug reaction (ADR)

An adverse drug reaction (ADR) is defined as any harmful or unwanted effect resulting from the use of a drug or medication. This can include side effects, allergic reactions, or other negative outcomes that occur after taking a medication. Adverse drug reactions can range from mild symptoms such as nausea or headaches, to more severe reactions such as anaphylaxis or organ damage.

B. Serious ADR

A serious adverse drug reaction **(SADR)** is an adverse drug reaction that results in death, hospitalization, disability, or other life-threatening conditions. These reactions are usually unexpected and require immediate medical attention.

C. Unexpected ADR

An unexpected adverse drug reaction is an adverse reaction that is not listed in the product information or package insert for a drug. These reactions are usually not anticipated based on the known safety profile of the drug and may be related to the dose, route of administration, or patient characteristics.

D. Suspected ADR

A suspected adverse drug reaction (SADR) is an adverse event that is reported or observed after drug administration, which may or may not be causally related to the drug. These events are reported to pharmacovigilance authorities for evaluation and monitoring.

E. Causality

Causality is the relationship between a drug and an adverse event. It refers to the likelihood that a drug caused a particular adverse event. Causality assessment is important in pharmacovigilance to determine whether a particular adverse event is related to the drug or not.

F. Severity

The severity of an adverse drug reaction refers to the intensity of the adverse event and its impact on the patient's health. Adverse drug reactions can be classified as mild, moderate, or severe based on the severity of the clinical manifestations.

G. Frequency

The frequency of an adverse drug reaction refers to the number of occurrences of the adverse event in a given population over a period of time. The frequency of an adverse event can be expressed as a percentage or a rate, and is an important consideration in pharmacovigilance to determine the risk-benefit profile of a drug.

H. Risk management plan (RMP)

A risk management plan is a comprehensive plan designed to identify, evaluate, and minimize the risks associated with the use of a drug. RMPs are required for certain drugs, particularly those with a high risk of adverse events, and are designed to ensure that the benefits of a drug outweigh the risks.

I. Signal detection

Signal detection is the process of identifying potential safety issues or new adverse events associated with a drug or medication. This can be done through various methods, including spontaneous reporting, literature review, and electronic health records.

J. Signal evaluation

Signal evaluation is the process of assessing the potential significance of a signal. This includes evaluating the strength of the evidence, the severity and frequency of the adverse event, and the potential impact on patient safety.

K. Signal refinement

Signal refinement is the process of further investigating and characterizing a signal to determine the need for additional regulatory action or changes to the drug's labeling or prescribing information.

Examples of basic terminologies used in pharmacovigilance include the adverse reactions associated with the use of thalidomide, a drug initially used to treat morning sickness in pregnant women. Thalidomide was found to cause severe birth defects, such as limb abnormalities and other malformations, in newborns whose mothers had taken the drug during pregnancy. The discovery of these adverse effects led to increased regulatory oversight and the development of stricter drug approval processes.

Another example is the unexpected adverse drug reactions associated with the use of the weight-loss drug fen-phen. Fen-phen was found to cause serious heart and lung complications such as primary pulmonary hypertension (PPH) and heart valve damage. The occurrence of these unexpected ADRs led to the withdrawal of fen-phen from the market in 1997. The link between fen-phen and PPH was identified through signal detection methods in pharmacovigilance, which involved analyzing post-marketing data on adverse events associated with the use of the drug. The signal was evaluated and confirmed through further investigations, leading to the identification of a causal relationship between fen-phen and PPH. The case of fen-phen underscores the importance of unexpected ADRs and the role of pharmacovigilance in detecting and managing them. By identifying and managing unexpected ADRs, pharmacovigilance plays a critical role in ensuring the safety and efficacy of medications and protecting public health.

B. Regulatory terminologies

Regulatory terminologies refer to the standardized definitions and classifications of adverse events used by regulatory agencies such as the FDA and the EMA. These terminologies help to facilitate communication and consistency in reporting of adverse events, which is essential for effective pharmacovigilance.

One important regulatory terminology is the MedDRA (Medical Dictionary for Regulatory Activities), which is a standardized medical terminology developed by the International Council for Harmonization of Technical Requirements for Pharmaceuticals for Human Use (ICH). MedDRA is used worldwide for the classification of adverse events in clinical trials, post-marketing surveillance, and regulatory reporting.

Another important terminology is the Common Terminology Criteria for Adverse Events (CTCAE), which is used by the National Cancer Institute (NCI) to grade the severity of adverse events in cancer clinical trials. The CTCAE provides standardized definitions and severity grades for a range of adverse events commonly associated with cancer therapies.

In addition to MedDRA and CTCAE, other regulatory terminologies include the WHO Adverse Reaction Terminology (WHO-ART), the International Classification of Diseases (ICD), and the Anatomical Therapeutic Chemical (ATC) classification system. These terminologies are used in various contexts, including pharmacovigilance, clinical trials, and healthcare billing.

Standardized regulatory terminologies are crucial for effective pharmacovigilance, as they allow for accurate and consistent reporting of adverse events across different studies and regulatory agencies. This helps to improve patient safety and ensure that drugs are used in a safe and effective manner.

XII

Drug and Disease Classification

Pharmacovigilance involves monitoring the safety and efficacy of drugs in the market to ensure that they are safe for human consumption. One important aspect of pharmacovigilance is the classification of drugs and diseases. The classification of drugs is essential in understanding their mechanisms of action, potential side effects, and interactions with other drugs. On the other hand, the classification of diseases helps in identifying the underlying conditions that may predispose individuals to adverse drug reactions and other drug-related problems. In this section, we will discuss the classification of drugs and diseases in pharmacovigilance.

12.1 Anatomical, therapeutic and chemical classification of drugs

In pharmacovigilance, drugs are classified according to their Anatomical, Therapeutic and Chemical (ATC) classification system. This system was developed by the World Health Organization (WHO) in collaboration with the Nordic Council on Medicines in the 1970s. The ATC system is used worldwide for the classification of drugs and is an important tool in the analysis of drug utilization and the monitoring of drug safety.

The ATC system is a hierarchical system, consisting of five levels of classification.

The first level is the anatomical main group, which is based on the organ or system on which the drug acts. This level is divided into 14 main groups, which include drugs that act on the nervous system, the cardiovascular system, and the digestive system, among others.

The second level of classification is the therapeutic subgroup, which is based on the therapeutic indication of the drug. This level is divided into more than 200 therapeutic subgroups, which include antihypertensive drugs, antidiabetic drugs, and antineoplastic drugs, among others.

The third level of classification is the pharmacological subgroup, which is based on the pharmacological mechanism of action of the drug. This level is divided into more than 1,000 pharmacological subgroups, which include beta-blocking agents, calcium channel blockers, and selective serotonin reuptake inhibitors (SSRIs), among others.

The fourth level of classification is the chemical subgroup, which is based on the chemical structure of the drug. This level is divided into more than 5,000 chemical subgroups, which include benzodiazepines, penicillins, and statins, among others.

The fifth level of classification is the chemical substance, which is the individual chemical compound that is responsible for the pharmacological effect of the drug. This level is identified by a unique 7-digit code assigned by the WHO Collaborating Centre for Drug Statistics Methodology.

The ATC classification system is useful in pharmacovigilance because it allows for the identification of drugs that are associated with specific adverse drug reactions (ADRs). By analyzing the data on ADRs associated with drugs in specific ATC subgroups or classes, pharmacovigilance professionals can identify potential safety concerns and take appropriate measures to minimize the risk of harm to patients.

12.2 International classification of diseases

The International Classification of Diseases (ICD) is a system used to classify and code diseases and health-related problems. The ICD is maintained by the World Health Organization (WHO) and is considered a standard classification system for healthcare and research purposes. The ICD is designed to promote international comparability and uniformity in the collection, processing, classification, and presentation of health statistics.

The ICD is periodically updated to reflect changes in medical knowledge, new diseases, and changes in health practices and technology. The latest version, ICD-11, was released in 2018 and includes several changes to the previous version, ICD-10.

In pharmacovigilance, the ICD system is used to classify adverse events and medical conditions reported during the use of medicinal products. Each adverse event is assigned a specific code from the ICD system, which allows for easy retrieval and analysis of data related to a particular condition or disease.

The ICD system is divided into chapters based on different disease categories, such as infectious and parasitic diseases, neoplasms, endocrine and metabolic disorders, and mental and behavioral disorders. Within each chapter, diseases are further classified based on their specific characteristics and clinical features. The ICD also includes codes for external causes of injury, such as accidents and violence, which are important in pharmacovigilance for identifying potential drug-related causes of injury or death.

The use of the ICD system in pharmacovigilance enables the collection and analysis of data on the incidence and prevalence of adverse events associated with specific medicinal products. This data can be used to identify potential safety concerns and inform regulatory decisions regarding the use and labeling of medicinal products. The ICD system is also useful for monitoring trends in adverse event reporting over time and identifying potential new safety signals.

The ICD system is an important tool in pharmacovigilance for the classification and coding of adverse events and medical conditions. It allows for easy retrieval and analysis of data related to specific diseases and conditions, which can inform regulatory decisions and improve patient safety.

12.3 *Daily defined doses* :

Daily Defined Dose (DDD) is a standardized measure of drug consumption used in pharmacovigilance to compare the use of different drugs or drug classes. The World Health Organization (WHO) established DDD as a measurement unit for drug utilization studies in 1976. The DDD is defined as the assumed average maintenance dose per day for a drug used for its main indication in adults.

The DDD is not intended to represent a recommended dose or a therapeutic dose for an individual patient, but rather it is a statistical tool used to estimate drug utilization patterns across different populations. It allows comparisons of drug utilization across populations, and enables identification of trends and changes in drug utilization patterns over time.

The calculation of DDDs is based on the anatomical, therapeutic, and chemical (ATC) classification system, which classifies drugs according to their indication, pharmacological class, and chemical structure. Each drug in the ATC system is assigned a unique five-level code, which includes a letter for the anatomical main group, a number for the therapeutic subgroup, and a letter for the chemical subgroup.

To calculate the DDD for a drug, a group of experts reviews the available scientific evidence on the drug's pharmacology, dosing, and therapeutic use. The experts use this information to estimate the average daily maintenance dose required to achieve the drug's therapeutic effect in adults. The DDD is then expressed in milligrams or other appropriate units of measurement.

The DDD has several applications in pharmacovigilance. It can be used to identify drugs or drug classes that are overused or underused, to monitor changes in prescribing patterns, to compare drug utilization across different regions or countries, and to detect potential safety issues associated with the use of a particular drug or drug class.

However, it is important to note that the DDD is not a perfect measure of drug utilization, and its usefulness in pharmacovigilance has some limitations. For example, it does not account for differences in drug efficacy or safety, nor does it consider differences in dosing requirements for different patient populations, such as children or elderly patients.

The DDD is a standardized measure of drug consumption used in pharmacovigilance to compare the use of different drugs or drug classes. It provides a useful tool for monitoring drug utilization patterns, identifying trends and changes in drug utilization over time, and detecting potential safety issues associated with the use of a particular drug or drug class. However, it is important to use the DDD in conjunction with other measures of drug utilization and to interpret the results in light of the drug's therapeutic efficacy and safety profile.

12.4 WHO adverse reaction terminologies

In pharmacovigilance, accurate and standardized terminology is essential for effective communication and assessment of adverse drug reactions (ADRs). To achieve this, the World Health Organization (WHO) has developed several terminologies for ADRs.

One of the most widely used terminologies is the Medical Dictionary for Regulatory Activities (MedDRA), which is a standardized international medical terminology used for regulatory purposes. MedDRA includes a hierarchical structure of terms, with high-level terms such as System Organ Class (SOC) and

Preferred Term (PT), which allow for easy classification and coding of ADRs.

Another important terminology is the WHO Adverse Reaction Terminology (WHO-ART), which is a standardized dictionary of medical terms used to describe adverse reactions to drugs. It includes a hierarchical structure of terms and allows for classification of ADRs based on body system, symptom, and severity.

The WHO also developed the Uppsala Monitoring Centre (UMC) causality assessment system, which is used to determine the likelihood that a particular drug caused a specific adverse event. The UMC system includes four categories of causality: certain, probable/likely, possible, and unlikely.

In addition to these terminologies, the WHO has also developed the International Classification of Diseases (ICD), which is used for the classification of diseases and health problems. The ICD provides a standardized system for coding and classifying health conditions, including those that are drug-related.

12.5 MedDRA and Standardized MedDRA queries

MedDRA (Medical Dictionary for Regulatory Activities) is a standardized medical terminology developed by the International Council for Harmonisation of Technical Requirements for Pharmaceuticals for Human Use (ICH) for the classification of adverse drug reactions (ADRs). It is widely used in pharmacovigilance to facilitate the collection, analysis, and dissemination of ADR data. MedDRA provides a standardized language for the description of medical events and has been endorsed by regulatory authorities worldwide.

MedDRA is organized into five levels of hierarchical terms. The first level, System Organ Class (SOC), contains 27 high-level categories that group related adverse events based on their affected organ system or physiological function. Examples of SOC include "General disorders and administration site conditions" and

"Nervous system disorders." The second level is the High-Level Group Term (HLGT), which further refines the SOC categories into more specific groupings. The third level is the High-Level Term (HLT), which provides a more specific description of the HLGT categories. The fourth level is the Preferred Term (PT), which is the lowest level of specificity in the MedDRA hierarchy and provides a detailed description of the medical event. The fifth level is the Lowest Level Term (LLT), which provides a more granular description of the PT.

In addition to MedDRA, Standardized MedDRA Queries (SMQs) have been developed to facilitate signal detection and data mining in pharmacovigilance. SMQs are pre-defined sets of MedDRA terms grouped together based on their clinical similarity and relevance to specific medical conditions or areas of interest. SMQs are designed to identify potential safety signals in a large database of ADR reports by identifying the frequency and pattern of MedDRA terms within the data.

SMQs are useful tools for safety signal detection and can be used in a variety of ways, including as an aid in case assessment, as a means of generating new hypotheses, and as a tool for identifying patterns of drug use and ADRs. They have been widely used in drug safety monitoring by regulatory authorities, pharmaceutical companies, and academic researchers.

12.6 *WHO drug dictionary*

The WHO Drug Dictionary is a reference tool that contains information on drugs and other substances used for medical purposes. It is maintained by the World Health Organization (WHO) and is used globally as a standard for drug information. The WHO Drug Dictionary is used extensively in pharmacovigilance and drug safety monitoring activities.

The WHO Drug Dictionary provides a standardized nomenclature for drugs, which enables easy identification and classification of drugs based on their chemical, therapeutic and pharmacological properties. The drug dictionary contains information on the active ingredients, dosage forms, route of administration, and strength of various drugs. It also includes information on generic names, trade names, and synonyms for drugs.

The WHO Drug Dictionary is available in multiple languages and is constantly updated to include new drugs and information. It is used in various electronic databases and information systems to ensure consistent identification and classification of drugs across different countries and regions.

In pharmacovigilance, the WHO Drug Dictionary is used for coding and classifying adverse drug reactions (ADRs) reported by healthcare professionals and patients. This helps in the analysis of ADR data to identify potential safety signals and to monitor the safety of drugs. The dictionary is also used to standardize drug information in clinical trials and in drug utilization studies.

The WHO Drug Dictionary has several advantages in pharmacovigilance and drug safety monitoring. It provides a common language for communication among healthcare professionals, regulatory authorities, and other stakeholders involved in drug safety monitoring. It also helps to standardize drug information and ensures that information on drugs is accurate and up-to-date. The use of the dictionary helps to improve the quality and consistency of ADR data and facilitates the timely identification of potential safety concerns associated with drugs.

The WHO Drug Dictionary is an essential tool in pharmacovigilance and drug safety monitoring activities. It provides a standardized nomenclature for drugs, which enables easy identification and classification of drugs based on their chemical, therapeutic, and pharmacological properties. The use of the dictionary helps to standardize drug information and ensures that information on drugs is accurate and up-to-date.

12.7 Eudravigilance medicinal product dictionary

The Eudravigilance Medicinal Product Dictionary (EVMPD) is a database managed by the European Medicines Agency (EMA) that contains information about medicinal products authorized for use in the European Union (EU). The database is a key tool for pharmacovigilance activities in the EU and is used to support the identification and monitoring of adverse drug reactions (ADRs) associated with the use of these products.

The EVMPD contains information on the active ingredients, strength, dosage form, route of administration, and other key characteristics of medicinal products authorized for use in the EU. This information is submitted by marketing authorization holders (MAHs) and is used by regulatory authorities and other stakeholders for a range of purposes, including signal detection, risk management, and post-authorization safety studies.

One of the main benefits of the EVMPD is that it provides a standardized and consistent approach to the recording and reporting of medicinal product information across the EU. This helps to ensure that all stakeholders have access to accurate and up-to-date information about the products that are being used in clinical practice. The database also facilitates the exchange of information between different regulatory authorities, which can help to improve the efficiency and effectiveness of pharmacovigilance activities across the EU.

The EVMPD plays a critical role in supporting pharmacovigilance activities in the EU and is an important tool for ensuring the safety of medicinal products used in clinical practice.

12.8 Information resources in pharmacovigilance

12.8.1 Basic drug information resources

Basic drug information resources are essential tools in pharmacovigilance to facilitate the identification and reporting of ADRs. They provide accurate, up-to-date information on drugs, including indications, dosage, adverse effects, contraindications, and interactions. Some of the basic drug information resources used in pharmacovigilance include:

Drug package inserts: These are written summaries of the essential information about a drug, including its approved indications, dosages, warnings, and adverse effects.

Drug formularies: These are comprehensive lists of drugs, usually arranged by therapeutic category or class, that provide information on indications, dosages, adverse effects, and contraindications.

Pharmacopoeias: These are authoritative compendia of drugs and pharmaceuticals that contain information on their properties, uses, dosages, and quality standards.

Textbooks and reference books: These are comprehensive sources of information on drugs and their uses, providing detailed information on drug interactions, adverse effects, and other important considerations.

Online databases: DailyMed, Drugs.com, and RxList are all online databases that provide comprehensive drug information resources. DailyMed is maintained by the National Library of Medicine and includes information on prescription and over-the-counter drugs, including dosage, administration, warnings, and potential side effects. Drugs.com offers information on drugs, supplements, and medical devices, as well as a pill identifier tool and drug interaction checker. RxList provides drug information, news, and a pill identifier tool. These online databases can be a valuable resource for healthcare professionals and patients to access accurate and up-to-date drug information. They can also assist in identifying potential adverse drug reactions and drug interactions. However, it is important to note that while these databases are a helpful resource, they should not replace consultation with a healthcare professional for individualized medical advice.

12.8.2 Specialized resources for ADRs

A.Pharmacovigilance databases

I. FDA Adverse Event Reporting System (FAERS)

The FDA Adverse Event Reporting System (FAERS) is a database that contains information on adverse events (AEs), medication errors, and product quality problems associated with FDA-regulated drugs and therapeutic biologic products. The database is managed by the FDA's Center for Drug Evaluation and Research (CDER) and contains over 12 million reports of adverse events and medication errors that have been submitted to the FDA since 1969.

The purpose of FAERS is to help the FDA identify potential safety concerns with drugs and biologics and to monitor the safety of these products once they are on the market. The information in FAERS is used to support various activities, such as:

Identifying new safety concerns: FAERS data can help the FDA identify previously unknown or poorly understood adverse events associated with a drug or biologic.

Evaluating known safety concerns: FAERS data can be used to evaluate the frequency, severity, and outcome of known adverse events associated with a drug or biologic.

Monitoring drug safety: FAERS data can be used to monitor the safety of a drug or biologic once it is on the market, as well as to evaluate the effectiveness of risk mitigation measures.

Access to FAERS is available to the public, and users can search the database for information on specific drugs, adverse events, and other variables. However, it is important to note that the data in FAERS is not intended to be used for comparative safety evaluations between drugs, as the data are subject to limitations and biases inherent in spontaneous reporting systems. FAERS data should be used in conjunction with other sources of drug safety information, such as clinical trials and observational studies.

II. European Medicines Agency (EMA) EudraVigilance

EudraVigilance is the European Medicines Agency's (EMA) database of suspected adverse drug reactions (ADRs) occurring in the European Economic Area (EEA). The database was established to provide a single point of entry for the reporting and analysis of suspected ADRs for all medicines authorized in the EEA.

Pharmaceutical companies, regulatory authorities, healthcare professionals, and patients can report suspected ADRs to EudraVigilance. The reports are evaluated by the EMA and national regulatory authorities to identify potential safety signals and take necessary regulatory actions, such as changes in the product information or restriction of the use of a medicine.

EudraVigilance also provides access to information on authorized medicines, including summaries of product characteristics (SmPCs), package leaflets, and product labeling. The database can be searched for information on individual medicines, active substances, and adverse reactions.

The EMA also provides other resources to support pharmacovigilance activities, such as the EudraGMDP database, which provides information on good manufacturing practices for medicines, and the EudraPharm database, which provides information on authorized medicines and their availability in the EEA.

III. World Health Organization (WHO) Global Individual Case Safety Report (ICSR) database

The WHO Global ICSR database is an online resource for pharmacovigilance that provides a centralized platform for the reporting and analysis of adverse drug reactions (ADRs) from around the world. The database is maintained by the Uppsala Monitoring Centre (UMC) in Sweden, which is a collaborating center of the WHO for drug safety. The Global ICSR database includes individual case safety reports (ICSRs) submitted by national pharmacovigilance centers, pharmaceutical companies, and healthcare professionals from over 130 countries. The reports contain detailed information on the patient, the drug(s) involved, the adverse event(s), and any other relevant medical history or concomitant medications. The WHO Global ICSR database is used by regulatory agencies, healthcare professionals, and pharmaceutical companies to monitor drug safety, identify potential safety concerns, and support risk management decisions. It is also used for research and analysis to better understand the safety profiles of medications and to identify patterns and trends in ADR reporting.

B. Medical literature databases

PubMed

PubMed is a free online database provided by the US National Library of Medicine (NLM) that contains millions of biomedical literature citations and abstracts from the MEDLINE database, as well as other life science journals and online books. It is an important resource for pharmacovigilance professionals as it allows them to search for relevant literature on adverse drug reactions (ADRs), drug interactions, drug safety, and other topics related to pharmacovigilance. PubMed also provides links to full-text articles and other related resources, making it a valuable tool for research and information gathering. It is widely used by healthcare professionals, researchers, and students around the world.

Embase

Embase is a biomedical and pharmacological database that provides comprehensive and up-to-date information on drugs, diseases, and medical devices. It includes over 32 million abstracts and citations from more than 8,500 international journals, as well as conference proceedings, books, and patents. Embase also covers information from grey literature, including regulatory documents, conference abstracts, and clinical trials reports.

Embase is widely used by pharmacovigilance professionals, researchers, and healthcare practitioners to retrieve relevant literature on adverse drug reactions, drug safety, drug interactions, and other pharmacological topics. It allows users to search for literature using advanced search tools, including MeSH terms, keywords, and Boolean operators, and provides various filters to refine the search results. Embase also offers a feature called Embase Alerts, which allows users to receive regular updates on new publications that match their search criteria.

In pharmacovigilance, Embase is often used in conjunction with other databases and resources, such as PubMed, to ensure comprehensive coverage of the literature on drug safety and adverse events. The information retrieved from Embase can help pharmacovigilance professionals to identify and evaluate potential safety signals and to develop strategies for managing and preventing adverse drug reactions.

C. Adverse drug reaction alert systems

I. MedWatch

MedWatch is the FDA's safety information and adverse event reporting program. It was established in 1993 to provide healthcare professionals and the public with timely access to important safety information on drugs and medical devices, and to facilitate the reporting of adverse events and medication errors. MedWatch offers several resources, including safety alerts, recalls, and public health advisories, as well as a platform for reporting adverse events. Healthcare professionals and consumers can submit reports of adverse events through the MedWatch Online Voluntary Reporting Form, the FDA Safety Information and Adverse Event Reporting Program, or by calling the FDA at 1-800-FDA-1088. The FDA encourages healthcare professionals and patients to report any adverse events associated with the use of drugs and medical devices, as it helps to identify and evaluate potential safety issues and improve patient care.

II. RxISK

RxISK is a free, independent drug safety website that allows patients, healthcare professionals, and researchers to report and analyze adverse drug reactions (ADRs). The website was founded by Dr. David Healy, a renowned psychiatrist and expert in psychopharmacology. RxISK provides a platform for individuals to report their experiences with medications, which are then analyzed by a team of experts to identify potential patterns and trends in ADRs. The website also offers a symptom checker tool, which helps users identify potential ADRs and provides information on how to report them to regulatory agencies. RxISK aims to increase transparency in drug safety by empowering patients and healthcare professionals to share their experiences and contribute to a global database of drug safety information.

D. Social media monitoring tools

Social media monitoring tools are becoming increasingly important in pharmacovigilance, as patients often share their experiences with medications on various social media platforms. These tools allow for the identification of potential adverse events that may not have been reported through traditional reporting channels. Some examples of social media monitoring tools used in pharmacovigilance include:

Advera Health Analytics - This tool analyzes social media and other online data sources to identify adverse events related to drugs and other medical products.

Epidemico - This platform collects and analyzes data from social media, news sources, and other online channels to identify potential adverse events related to drugs and other medical products.

HealthUnlocked - This social media platform provides a space for patients to connect with others who have similar health conditions and share their experiences with medications.

PatientsLikeMe - This online community allows patients to track their health and medication use and share their experiences with others who have similar conditions.

XIII
Establishing Pharmacovigilance Program

The establishment of a pharmacovigilance program is critical for ensuring the safety and efficacy of medicinal products, and the implementation of such a program requires a coordinated effort involving various stakeholders, including regulatory authorities, healthcare providers, pharmaceutical companies, and patients.

13.1 Establishing in a hospital

Establishing a pharmacovigilance program in a hospital is essential to ensure the safe and effective use of medicines. The program helps in detecting, assessing, understanding, and preventing any adverse drug reactions or drug-related problems. Hospitals have a crucial role to play in pharmacovigilance as they are responsible for the administration of medicines to patients.

The first step in establishing a pharmacovigilance program in a hospital is to form a pharmacovigilance committee. This committee should comprise members from different departments of the hospital, such as pharmacy, medicine, nursing, and administration. The committee should have a clear objective and should be responsible for overseeing the implementation of the pharmacovigilance program.

The committee should conduct regular training programs for healthcare professionals in the hospital. The training should focus on identifying and reporting adverse drug reactions, understanding the importance of pharmacovigilance, and using appropriate terminology for reporting adverse events.

The hospital should also establish a system for reporting adverse drug reactions. This system should be easily accessible to all healthcare professionals and should provide clear guidelines on how to report adverse events. The reports should be promptly collected, evaluated, and documented to identify any patterns or trends in adverse drug reactions.

The hospital should have a mechanism to share information about adverse drug reactions with relevant authorities, such as the national pharmacovigilance center, drug regulatory authorities, and other hospitals. This sharing of information can help in identifying the safety profile of medicines and implementing necessary measures to prevent adverse drug reactions.

Regular monitoring and evaluation of the pharmacovigilance program in the hospital is essential. The program's effectiveness should be assessed periodically by the pharmacovigilance committee, and necessary changes should be made to improve the program's efficiency.

13.2 Establishment & operation of drug safety department in industry

Pharmacovigilance is an essential component of the drug development process, and it is mandatory for pharmaceutical companies to establish a drug safety department to ensure the safety and effectiveness of their products. The drug safety department is responsible for implementing and managing pharmacovigilance activities for the company's marketed products and investigational drugs.

The establishment and operation of a drug safety department in the pharmaceutical industry involve several steps. The first step is to identify the roles and responsibilities of the department, which may vary depending on the company's size and organizational structure. The drug safety department should have adequate resources, including staff and budget, to carry out its functions effectively. It is essential to establish a clear reporting structure to ensure that the department's activities are integrated with other departments within the organization.

The drug safety department should have a qualified and trained staff with expertise in pharmacovigilance, epidemiology, statistics, and regulatory affairs. The staff should be trained in pharmacovigilance processes, including the identification, evaluation, and reporting of adverse drug reactions (ADRs), as well as regulatory requirements and guidelines. The department should also establish standard operating procedures (SOPs) for pharmacovigilance activities, which should be regularly reviewed and updated.

The drug safety department is responsible for the timely and accurate collection, evaluation, and reporting of ADRs associated with the company's products. This includes monitoring the safety of marketed products through post-marketing surveillance studies, clinical trials, and spontaneous reports from healthcare professionals and patients. The department should also ensure compliance with regulatory reporting requirements and guidelines, including expedited reporting of serious and unexpected ADRs.

In addition to pharmacovigilance activities, the drug safety department should also be involved in risk management activities, such as developing risk management plans and implementing risk minimization measures. The department should also provide drug safety information and training to internal and external stakeholders, including healthcare professionals and patients.

To ensure the effective operation of the drug safety department, it is essential to establish a quality management system (QMS) that includes regular audits, inspections, and quality control measures.

The QMS should be designed to ensure the accuracy, completeness, and reliability of pharmacovigilance data, as well as compliance with regulatory requirements and guidelines.

13.3 Contract Research Organizations (CROs)

Contract Research Organizations (CROs) are companies that provide research services to pharmaceutical and biotechnology companies. They assist these companies in the drug development process by conducting clinical trials, collecting and analyzing data, and providing regulatory support. CROs play a crucial role in the pharmaceutical industry as they allow drug companies to outsource their research and development activities to specialized organizations.

In the context of pharmacovigilance, CROs can provide services such as safety monitoring, data management, signal detection, and risk management. These services can help pharmaceutical companies meet regulatory requirements and ensure the safety and efficacy of their products.

Establishing a pharmacovigilance program in a CRO involves several steps. First, the CRO must establish a drug safety department that is responsible for all aspects of pharmacovigilance. This department should have qualified personnel with expertise in pharmacovigilance, drug safety, and regulatory affairs. The department should also have a well-defined organizational structure with clear roles and responsibilities.

The next step is to develop standard operating procedures (SOPs) for pharmacovigilance activities. These SOPs should cover all aspects of pharmacovigilance, including adverse event reporting, signal detection, risk management, and quality management. The SOPs should be reviewed and updated regularly to ensure that they are up-to-date and comply with regulatory requirements.

CROs also need to have appropriate systems in place for data collection, management, and analysis. This includes a pharmacovigilance database that is capable of collecting and storing adverse event data from multiple sources, including clinical trials, post-marketing surveillance, and literature reports. The database should also have tools for data analysis and signal detection.

In addition, CROs need to have a well-trained and qualified pharmacovigilance team that can provide accurate and timely safety assessments of adverse events. This includes medical review of adverse events, assessment of causality, severity, and expectedness, and the development of risk management plans.

Finally, CROs must ensure that their pharmacovigilance program complies with regulatory requirements in the countries where they operate. This includes compliance with local pharmacovigilance regulations, submission of timely and accurate reports to regulatory authorities, and participation in regulatory inspections and audits.

13.4 Establishing a national programme

Establishing a pharmacovigilance program is crucial to ensure the safe and effective use of medicines. National pharmacovigilance programs can be established to monitor and evaluate the safety of medicines in a country. These programs involve the collection, analysis, and interpretation of data on adverse drug reactions (ADRs) to ensure that the benefits of a medicine outweigh its risks. Here are some steps that can be taken to establish a national pharmacovigilance program:

Legal framework: The first step in establishing a pharmacovigilance program is to create a legal framework that outlines the roles and responsibilities of all stakeholders involved in the program. This includes establishing a regulatory body responsible for overseeing the program, as well as guidelines for reporting ADRs.

Reporting system: A reporting system should be established to allow healthcare professionals and patients to report ADRs. This system should be accessible and easy to use, and reports should be confidential and anonymous to encourage reporting.

Data collection and analysis: Once ADRs are reported, data should be collected and analyzed to identify potential safety issues with medicines. This data can be used to generate signals that may indicate a safety issue with a medicine, which can then be investigated further.

Risk management: Risk management strategies should be developed for medicines that are associated with significant risks. This may include changes to product labeling or restrictions on the use of a medicine.

Communication: Effective communication is essential for the success of a pharmacovigilance program. Healthcare professionals, patients, and the general public should be informed about the program and the importance of reporting ADRs.

Capacity building: Capacity building is important to ensure that the program is sustainable in the long term. This may involve training healthcare professionals on pharmacovigilance principles and best practices, as well as providing resources to support the program.

Establishing a national pharmacovigilance program can be a challenging process, but it is an essential step in ensuring the safe and effective use of medicines. By following these steps, countries can establish a program that is effective, sustainable, and responsive to the needs of patients and healthcare professionals.

XIV
Vaccine Safety Surveillance

14.1 Vaccine pharmacovigilance

Vaccines are crucial for the prevention and control of infectious diseases, and their safety and efficacy are of paramount importance. Vaccines undergo rigorous testing and regulatory approval processes before they are licensed for use in the general population. However, even after approval, continuous monitoring of vaccine safety is necessary to identify any potential adverse events following immunization (AEFIs).

Vaccine pharmacovigilance is the process of monitoring and evaluating the safety of vaccines throughout their life cycle, including post-licensure surveillance, signal detection, risk assessment, and risk management. The primary objective of vaccine pharmacovigilance is to ensure that vaccines are safe and effective, and any AEFIs are identified and managed promptly.

There are several systems in place for vaccine pharmacovigilance, including passive and active surveillance systems. Passive surveillance systems rely on spontaneous reporting of AEFIs by healthcare professionals, patients, or their caregivers. These reports are collected and analyzed to identify potential safety signals. The primary limitation of passive surveillance systems is that they rely on voluntary reporting, and there may be underreporting or reporting bias.

Active surveillance systems, on the other hand, involve actively monitoring individuals who receive vaccines and comparing their health outcomes with a control group. These systems can be more effective in detecting rare or unexpected AEFIs. Examples of active surveillance systems include vaccine safety datalink, the Clinical Immunization Safety Assessment network, and the Global Vaccine Safety Initiative.

In addition to these surveillance systems, vaccine pharmacovigilance also involves signal detection and risk assessment. Signal detection refers to the identification of potential safety signals based on the analysis of data from various sources, including clinical trials, post-marketing surveillance, and epidemiological studies. Risk assessment involves the evaluation of the potential risks associated with a vaccine and the determination of the overall benefit-risk profile.

Risk management is another critical component of vaccine pharmacovigilance. Once a safety signal is detected, risk management strategies may be implemented to minimize the risk of AEFIs. These strategies may include changes in vaccine formulation, product labeling, or vaccination schedules, or even withdrawal of the vaccine from the market.

14.2 Vaccination failure

Vaccination is a highly effective strategy to prevent infectious diseases, but it is not 100% effective. The failure of vaccination, also known as vaccine failure, refers to the inability of a vaccine to provide immunity or protect against a particular infectious disease. The reasons for vaccine failure can be complex and multifactorial, and can occur at different stages of the vaccination process.

One of the main reasons for vaccine failure is related to the immune response of the vaccinated individual. Vaccines work by stimulating the immune system to produce a protective response against a specific pathogen. However, some people may not mount a sufficient immune response to the vaccine, either due to underlying health conditions, genetic factors, or other factors that impair the immune system. In some cases, the effectiveness of a vaccine may also decrease over time, requiring booster doses to maintain immunity.

Another reason for vaccine failure is related to the pathogen itself. Some pathogens, such as the influenza virus, can mutate rapidly, leading to the emergence of new strains that are not covered by existing vaccines. In such cases, the development of new vaccines may be necessary to provide protection against the new strains.

Other factors that can contribute to vaccine failure include errors in vaccine administration, such as incorrect storage or handling of the vaccine, as well as individual behaviors that increase the risk of exposure to the pathogen. For example, a person who is vaccinated against a sexually transmitted infection but engages in unprotected sexual activity may still be at risk of infection.

Vaccine failure can have significant public health implications, particularly in the context of infectious disease outbreaks. When a significant proportion of the population is not immune to a particular pathogen, either due to vaccine failure or lack of vaccination, the pathogen can spread rapidly, leading to outbreaks and epidemics. In some cases, vaccine failure can also contribute to the emergence of vaccine-resistant strains of pathogens, which can be more difficult to treat and control.

Pharmacovigilance plays an important role in monitoring and managing vaccine failure. By collecting and analyzing data on adverse events following vaccination, pharmacovigilance systems can help identify patterns of vaccine failure and other safety concerns related to vaccines. This information can be used to improve vaccine design and administration, as well as to inform public health policies aimed at increasing vaccination coverage and reducing the risk of infectious disease outbreaks.

14.3 Adverse events following immunization

Adverse events following immunization (AEFIs) refer to any untoward medical occurrence that follows immunization, whether or not it is causally related to the vaccination. AEFIs are a critical concern in vaccine pharmacovigilance as they can have significant consequences, both for individuals and for public health programs.

AEFIs can range from mild, such as local reactions at the injection site, to severe, such as anaphylaxis, encephalopathy, or death. The severity of AEFIs can vary depending on factors such as the age and underlying health status of the vaccine recipient, the type and dose of the vaccine, and the presence of other medical conditions.

The detection and reporting of AEFIs is a crucial component of vaccine pharmacovigilance. In many countries, national immunization programs have established surveillance systems to monitor AEFIs and ensure that vaccines are safe and effective. These surveillance systems rely on healthcare providers to report suspected AEFIs to local health authorities, who in turn report to national pharmacovigilance centers. The data collected through these systems help to identify potential safety signals and inform decisions about the continued use of vaccines.

In addition to passive surveillance systems, active surveillance methods such as vaccine safety studies can also be used to identify and evaluate AEFIs. These studies involve monitoring a large population of vaccine recipients for a defined period to assess the incidence of AEFIs and determine whether they are causally related to the vaccine. This type of research can help to provide more accurate estimates of the risk of AEFIs and can be used to identify populations at increased risk.

Preventing AEFIs is an important goal of vaccine pharmacovigilance. This can be achieved through several strategies, including ensuring that only safe and effective vaccines are licensed and distributed, providing appropriate vaccine education and counseling to individuals and healthcare providers, and developing and implementing effective vaccine safety monitoring and management protocols. In the event of an AEFI, appropriate medical management should be provided promptly, and the event should be reported to the relevant authorities to ensure that appropriate measures can be taken to minimize the risk of similar events in the future.

AEFIs are a critical concern in vaccine pharmacovigilance, and the detection, reporting, and prevention of AEFIs are essential to ensure the safety and effectiveness of vaccines. Through effective vaccine safety monitoring and management, we can continue to protect public health and prevent the spread of vaccine-preventable diseases.

XV
Pharmacovigilance Methods

15.1 Passive surveillance – Spontaneous reports and case series :

Pharmacovigilance methods aim to monitor the safety of medicines and minimize the risks associated with their use. Passive surveillance is one of the widely used methods for detecting and reporting adverse drug reactions (ADRs). In passive surveillance, the reporting of ADRs is voluntary, and healthcare professionals, patients, and pharmaceutical companies report ADRs to the national pharmacovigilance center.

The spontaneous reporting system (SRS) is the most commonly used form of passive surveillance. The SRS consists of collecting, evaluating, and archiving ADR reports from various sources. These sources include healthcare professionals, patients, and pharmaceutical companies. The SRS has the advantage of being cost-effective and easy to implement. The SRS reports are mainly used for signal detection, which helps to identify potential new risks associated with the use of drugs.

Case series is another form of passive surveillance that involves the collection and analysis of data from a group of patients who have experienced a similar ADR after exposure to a particular drug. Case series provide valuable information about the frequency, severity, and clinical features of ADRs associated with a particular drug. They also help to identify potential risk factors for ADRs.

However, passive surveillance has several limitations. Underreporting is a significant limitation of passive surveillance. Healthcare professionals and patients may not report all ADRs, leading to an underestimation of the true incidence of ADRs. There is also a lack of information on the denominator (the total number of patients exposed to a drug), which makes it difficult to calculate the true incidence of ADRs. Moreover, the quality of the reports may vary, and the reports may not provide sufficient information to establish causality.

15.2 Stimulated reporting

Stimulated reporting is a method used in pharmacovigilance to increase the number of adverse drug reactions (ADRs) reported by healthcare professionals and patients. The goal of stimulated reporting is to encourage the reporting of suspected ADRs that might not otherwise be reported due to factors such as lack of knowledge, time constraints, or lack of awareness.

One of the methods used in stimulated reporting is educational interventions, such as training sessions and educational material distribution, aimed at increasing awareness of the importance of reporting ADRs. These interventions can target healthcare professionals, patients, or both. For example, educational interventions for healthcare professionals may include lectures, workshops, or online courses on pharmacovigilance and ADR reporting.

Another method used in stimulated reporting is providing feedback to reporters. This involves providing information to reporters about the outcomes of their reported ADRs, such as whether their report led to a change in the product information or a regulatory action. Feedback can be provided through newsletters, bulletins, or other communication channels.

Incentives can also be used to stimulate reporting. These may include rewards for reporters, such as recognition or financial incentives, or penalties for non-reporting. Financial incentives may be in the form of grants or funding to healthcare facilities or organizations that report a high number of ADRs.

Electronic reporting systems can also be used to stimulate reporting. These systems make it easier and more efficient for healthcare professionals and patients to report ADRs. Electronic reporting systems can provide automatic feedback to reporters and enable the monitoring of reporting rates, allowing for targeted interventions to increase reporting.

Stimulated reporting has been shown to be effective in increasing the number of ADR reports. However, it is important to note that this method may also lead to an increase in the reporting of non-serious or unlikely ADRs, which can result in unnecessary regulatory actions and resource allocation. Therefore, it is important to carefully evaluate the benefits and risks of using stimulated reporting methods and to ensure that the reporting system is able to appropriately assess the causality and severity of reported ADRs.

15.3 Active surveillance – Sentinel sites, drug event monitoring and registries

Active surveillance is a pharmacovigilance method that involves actively monitoring the safety of medicines or vaccines. Unlike passive surveillance, where adverse events are reported voluntarily by healthcare professionals and patients, active surveillance methods involve the systematic collection of data on adverse events from a defined population or sample.

One example of active surveillance is sentinel site surveillance. This involves selecting specific healthcare facilities, such as hospitals or clinics, to monitor for adverse events related to a specific medicine or vaccine. Data is collected from these facilities on a regular basis and analyzed to identify any trends or signals of potential safety concerns.

Another active surveillance method is drug event monitoring. This involves monitoring a specific population of patients who have been prescribed a particular medicine or vaccine. Data is collected through regular follow-up visits or questionnaires, and any adverse events are recorded and analyzed. This method allows for a more targeted approach to monitoring the safety of a specific medicine or vaccine.

Registries are also a form of active surveillance. These are databases that collect information on a specific population of patients who have been exposed to a particular medicine or vaccine. Registries may be disease-specific or drug-specific and can provide valuable information on the long-term safety of medicines or vaccines.

Active surveillance methods have several advantages over passive surveillance. They allow for a more targeted approach to monitoring the safety of medicines or vaccines, and can provide more detailed information on specific populations or medicines. They also allow for more proactive monitoring, as adverse events can be identified and acted upon more quickly.

However, active surveillance methods can also be more resource-intensive and may require a larger investment in terms of time and funding. Additionally, the populations being monitored may not be representative of the wider population, which can limit the generalizability of the findings.

15.4 *Comparative observational studies – Cross sectional study, case control study and cohort study*

Comparative observational studies are a type of research study used in pharmacovigilance to compare the incidence of adverse drug reactions (ADRs) between different groups of patients. There are three main types of comparative observational studies: cross-sectional studies, case-control studies, and cohort studies.

A. Cross-sectional studies

Cross-sectional study is a type of observational research design that aims to gather data from a population or a representative sample at a specific point in time. In this type of study, researchers collect information on the exposure and the outcome of interest simultaneously. The primary objective of a cross-sectional study is to provide an estimate of the prevalence of a particular disease or condition within a defined population.

Cross-sectional studies can be used to examine a wide range of research questions, including the prevalence of adverse drug reactions (ADRs) within a population, the distribution of risk factors for a particular disease or condition, and the patterns of healthcare utilization within a population. These studies are often conducted using surveys or interviews to collect data on the variables of interest.

One of the advantages of cross-sectional studies is that they can be relatively quick and inexpensive to conduct, as data can be collected from a large number of individuals at once. Additionally, these studies can be used to generate hypotheses for further research. However, a major limitation of cross-sectional studies is that they cannot establish cause-and-effect relationships between the exposure and the outcome of interest, as data are collected at a single point in time.

B. Case-control studies

Case-control studies are another method used in pharmacovigilance to evaluate the association between a drug and a specific adverse event. In this study design, cases with the adverse event of interest are identified and compared to a control group without the adverse event. The cases and controls are then evaluated for exposure to the drug in question. The odds ratio is calculated to determine the association between the drug and the adverse event.

Case-control studies are often used when the adverse event of interest is rare or has a long latency period. They can also be used when randomized controlled trials are not feasible or ethical. However, case-control studies are susceptible to selection bias, information bias, and confounding. To minimize bias, cases and controls should be carefully selected and matched based on relevant characteristics such as age, gender, and underlying medical conditions. Additionally, data should be collected from reliable sources such as medical records and standardized questionnaires.

Case-control studies have been used in pharmacovigilance to evaluate the association between drugs and adverse events such as acute liver injury with the use of statins, and the risk of major bleeding events with the use of anticoagulants. Results from case-control studies can help inform regulatory decisions regarding drug safety and can also guide prescribing practices for healthcare providers.

C. Cohort studies

Cohort studies are a type of observational study that involves the identification of a group of individuals who are exposed to a particular drug or intervention, and then following them over time to determine if they develop any adverse effects or outcomes. Cohort studies can be either prospective or retrospective, and they are often used to assess the safety and effectiveness of medications and other medical interventions.

In a prospective cohort study, a group of individuals who are exposed to a particular drug or intervention are identified and followed forward in time to see if they develop any adverse effects or outcomes. Data is collected at regular intervals during the study period, and any adverse events that occur are documented and analyzed. Prospective cohort studies are considered the gold standard for observational studies because they allow for the identification of cause-and-effect relationships between exposure to a drug or intervention and the development of adverse effects.

In a retrospective cohort study, a group of individuals who have been exposed to a particular drug or intervention in the past are identified and their medical records are reviewed to determine if they developed any adverse effects or outcomes. Retrospective cohort studies can be more challenging to conduct than prospective studies because they require the collection of data from medical records and other sources that may not be complete or accurate.

Cohort studies are particularly useful for identifying rare adverse events or outcomes that may not be detected in clinical trials or other types of studies. They can also be used to evaluate the long-term safety and effectiveness of medications and other medical interventions, and to identify factors that may increase the risk of adverse events or outcomes. However, cohort studies can be expensive and time-consuming to conduct, and they may be subject to bias or confounding factors that can affect the validity of the results.

15.5 Targeted clinical investigations

Targeted clinical investigations are an important aspect of pharmacovigilance. These investigations are conducted to gather more information about the safety and efficacy of a drug, particularly after it has been approved for use in the market. Targeted clinical investigations can be initiated by regulatory authorities, pharmaceutical companies, or independent researchers.

The aim of targeted clinical investigations is to assess the risk-benefit profile of a drug in real-world settings. These investigations are often designed to answer specific questions related to drug safety and effectiveness. For example, a targeted clinical investigation may be conducted to evaluate the risk of a specific adverse event associated with a drug, or to determine the effectiveness of a drug in a particular patient population.

There are several types of targeted clinical investigations, including post-marketing surveillance studies, phase IV trials, and observational studies. Post-marketing surveillance studies are conducted after a drug has been approved for use and are designed to monitor the safety and effectiveness of the drug in a real-world setting. Phase IV trials are also conducted after a drug has been approved, but they are designed to gather additional information about the drug's safety, efficacy, and optimal use. Observational studies, on the other hand, are designed to evaluate the safety and effectiveness of a drug in a specific patient population.

Targeted clinical investigations are essential for ensuring the safety and efficacy of drugs in the market. By gathering more information about a drug's risk-benefit profile, targeted clinical investigations can help identify potential safety issues and inform clinical practice guidelines. Additionally, these investigations can help optimize the use of a drug, by identifying patient populations that may benefit most from the drug.

Targeted clinical investigations are a critical component of pharmacovigilance. These investigations are designed to gather more information about the safety and effectiveness of drugs in real-world settings, and can help identify potential safety issues and optimize the use of drugs.

XVI
Communication in Pharmacovigilance

Communication is a critical component of pharmacovigilance. It is the process of exchanging information among various stakeholders, including healthcare providers, patients, regulatory agencies, and pharmaceutical companies. Effective communication is necessary to ensure timely and accurate reporting of adverse drug reactions (ADRs) and other drug-related events. This essay will discuss the importance of effective communication in pharmacovigilance, communication in drug safety crisis management, and communicating with regulatory agencies, business partners, healthcare facilities, and media.

16.1: Effective communication in Pharmacovigilance

Effective communication is a critical component of pharmacovigilance, as it is crucial to ensure that all stakeholders have access to timely and accurate information on drug safety. This includes healthcare providers, regulatory agencies, pharmaceutical companies, patients, and the general public. Failure to communicate effectively in pharmacovigilance can result in serious consequences, such as delayed identification of adverse drug reactions (ADRs), inadequate risk management, and lack of patient trust in the healthcare system.

One example of the importance of effective communication in pharmacovigilance is the case of the drug rosiglitazone, marketed under the trade name Avandia. In 2007, a meta-analysis published in the New England Journal of Medicine raised concerns about the cardiovascular safety of the drug. However, it was not until 2010 that the FDA required a black box warning on the drug's label, citing increased risk of heart attacks and strokes. The delay in communicating this critical safety information to healthcare providers and patients led to a prolonged period of inadequate risk management, potentially putting patients at risk.

Effective communication in pharmacovigilance involves several key elements.

1. It is important to establish clear and effective channels of communication between all stakeholders involved in drug safety. This includes healthcare providers, regulatory agencies, pharmaceutical companies, patients, and the media. These channels may include newsletters, websites, conferences, and other forms of communication.

2. It is important to ensure that communication is timely and accurate. This means that information on drug safety profiles, updates on ADRs, and other relevant information should be communicated as soon as possible to ensure that healthcare providers and patients are informed and able to make informed decisions.

3. Communication should be tailored to the specific needs of each stakeholder group. For example, healthcare providers may need more detailed information on drug safety profiles and ADRs, while patients may need more accessible and easy-to-understand information on how to recognize and report ADRs.

4. Effective communication in pharmacovigilance should be transparent and open. This means that stakeholders should be encouraged to report ADRs and provide feedback on drug safety

information, and that this feedback should be taken into account in decision-making processes.

5. Effective communication in pharmacovigilance involves ongoing evaluation and improvement of communication strategies. This means that communication channels and strategies should be regularly evaluated to ensure that they are effective in reaching all stakeholders and providing timely and accurate information.

16.2 Communication in Drug Safety Crisis management

Effective communication is crucial in drug safety crisis management to ensure that all stakeholders are informed and can work together to mitigate risks and prevent harm to patients. During a drug safety crisis, timely and accurate communication is essential to prevent panic and confusion, maintain trust in the healthcare system, and ultimately save lives.

One recent example of effective communication in drug safety crisis management is the response to the COVID-19 pandemic. In the early stages of the pandemic, there was a rapid development of vaccines to prevent the spread of the virus. However, concerns about vaccine safety arose, which could have led to vaccine hesitancy and a delay in vaccination efforts. Effective communication was essential to address these concerns and ensure that the public had accurate information about the safety and efficacy of the vaccines.

Regulatory agencies such as the US Food and Drug Administration (FDA) and the European Medicines Agency (EMA) played a critical role in providing updates on vaccine safety profiles, communicating the results of clinical trials, and addressing concerns about adverse events associated with the vaccines. They used various communication channels, including press releases, public statements, and social media, to disseminate information to the public, healthcare providers, and other stakeholders.

Pharmaceutical companies also played a vital role in effective communication during the COVID-19 pandemic. They provided information on the safety and efficacy of their vaccines and worked closely with regulatory agencies to ensure that their products met regulatory standards. Additionally, they collaborated with healthcare providers and patient advocacy groups to address concerns and provide accurate information to the public.

Effective communication in drug safety crisis management is not only important during the COVID-19 pandemic but also in other drug safety crises. For example, in 2004, there was a significant drug safety crisis involving the withdrawal of the painkiller Vioxx due to an increased risk of heart attacks and strokes. The withdrawal of Vioxx affected millions of patients worldwide and highlighted the importance of effective communication in drug safety crisis management. The pharmaceutical company Merck, which manufactured Vioxx, communicated regularly with healthcare providers and the public about the safety issues associated with the drug and provided information on alternative treatment options.

16.3 Communicating with Regulatory Agencies, Business Partners, Healthcare Facilities & Media

Effective communication with regulatory agencies, business partners, healthcare facilities, and the media is essential in pharmacovigilance. Regulatory agencies are responsible for evaluating drug safety and efficacy and may require additional safety data or risk management plans to ensure the safety of patients. Effective communication with regulatory agencies can help to ensure that safety concerns are identified and addressed promptly.

Business partners, including pharmaceutical companies and contract research organizations, play a critical role in pharmacovigilance. Effective communication with business partners is essential to ensure that safety data is collected, analyzed, and reported in a timely and accurate manner.

Healthcare facilities are often the first point of contact for patients who experience adverse drug reactions. Effective communication with healthcare facilities can help to ensure that ADRs are reported promptly and accurately. It can also facilitate the dissemination of drug safety information to healthcare providers, which can help to improve patient safety.

The media plays a crucial role in communicating drug safety information to the public. Effective communication with the media can help to ensure that accurate and timely information is disseminated to the public, which can help to build trust in drug safety systems.

It is essential to establish clear communication channels and protocols with all stakeholders involved in pharmacovigilance. This includes establishing standard operating procedures for reporting ADRs and communicating safety information. It is also essential to ensure that all stakeholders are aware of their roles and responsibilities and understand the importance of effective communication in ensuring patient safety.

XVII

Safety Data Generation & Statistical methods for Evaluating medication safety data

17.1 Introduction

A. Definition of medication safety data evaluation

Medication safety data evaluation refers to the process of assessing and analyzing the safety data of a drug after its approval and marketing. It involves monitoring the safety of a drug in real-world settings, detecting and assessing adverse events, and evaluating the effectiveness of risk minimization measures. The purpose of medication safety data evaluation is to ensure that a drug's benefits continue to outweigh its risks over time.

B. Importance of statistical methods in evaluating medication safety data

Statistical methods play a critical role in the evaluation of medication safety data. They provide a systematic approach to analyzing and interpreting large amounts of safety data, allowing researchers to identify patterns and trends that may not be apparent otherwise. Statistical methods can be used to detect adverse events, assess their severity and frequency, and evaluate the effectiveness of risk management strategies. They can also be used to compare the safety profiles of different drugs or different formulations of the same drug.

Statistical methods are particularly important in post-marketing surveillance studies, where large amounts of safety data are collected from multiple sources over an extended period. These studies often involve observational data, which can be subject to various biases and confounding factors. Statistical methods can help to control for these factors and provide more accurate estimates of the risks associated with a drug.

17.2 Importance of safety data generation in Pre-clinical phase

The pre-clinical phase is a critical stage in drug development because it provides the foundational data that informs the decision to move forward with clinical trials. The preclinical data provides a basis for establishing a drug's safety and efficacy profile, which is crucial for obtaining regulatory approval to move to the next stage of clinical development. Generating safety data during the preclinical phase is important because it can help identify potential toxicities that may impact patient safety and provide insights into the potential risk-benefit balance of the drug candidate.

The preclinical phase involves several stages of safety data generation, including in vitro and in vivo testing. In vitro testing involves using cells and tissues to evaluate the potential toxicity and efficacy of the drug candidate. This stage helps to identify the drug's mechanism of action, determine the optimal dosing regimen, and assess potential drug interactions. In vivo testing involves evaluating the drug's efficacy and safety in animal models, and assessing its pharmacokinetic profile, including absorption, distribution, metabolism, and elimination. This stage helps to identify any potential toxicities that may impact human subjects during clinical trials.

The data generated during the preclinical phase is critical for assessing the drug's safety and efficacy profile, identifying potential risks, and informing the design of subsequent clinical trials. Preclinical data can also help identify the optimal dosing regimen and route of administration, and inform the development of monitoring and safety protocols for use in clinical trials. Additionally, preclinical data can be used to support regulatory submissions for approval to initiate clinical trials and can help to mitigate risks associated with adverse events during clinical development.

17.3. Safety Data Generation in Pre-clinical Phase

17.3.1 In Vitro Studies

In vitro studies are an essential component of safety data generation in the pre-clinical phase of drug development. These studies involve the use of cell culture models, microbial studies, and enzyme assays to evaluate the safety of a potential drug candidate. In vitro studies are conducted prior to animal studies and clinical trials to identify potential safety issues early in the drug development process.

Cell culture studies involve the use of human or animal cells to evaluate the toxicity of a drug candidate. These studies can be used to determine the effect of a drug on various organs and tissues, including the liver, kidney, and heart. Researchers can use cell culture studies to identify potential safety concerns and assess the impact of a drug on specific cell types.

Microbial studies involve the use of microorganisms to evaluate the safety of a drug candidate. These studies can be used to determine the effect of a drug on bacteria and other microorganisms in the body. Microbial studies are particularly important for the development of antibiotics and other drugs that target bacterial infections.

Enzyme assays involve the use of enzymes to evaluate the safety of a drug candidate. These studies can be used to determine the effect of a drug on specific enzymes in the body. Enzyme assays are particularly important for the development of drugs that target specific metabolic pathways or enzymes.

17.3.2. In vivo studies

In vivo studies involve the use of live animals to assess the potential toxicological effects of a drug candidate. These studies are typically conducted in a stepwise manner, starting with acute toxicity studies and progressing to chronic toxicity studies. The purpose of these studies is to determine the safe dose range for the drug candidate and to identify any potential adverse effects that may occur at higher doses.

Acute toxicity studies are typically the first in vivo studies conducted during the pre-clinical phase. These studies are designed to assess the potential toxicity of a single dose of the drug candidate administered to animals. The animals are observed for a period of 24 to 72 hours after dosing to identify any signs of toxicity. The acute toxicity study provides important information about the potential toxic effects of the drug candidate and helps to identify the safe starting dose for subsequent studies.

Sub-acute toxicity studies are conducted to evaluate the potential toxicological effects of the drug candidate when administered over a period of 14 to 28 days. The animals are dosed daily, and they are observed for signs of toxicity and any changes in body weight or organ function. These studies provide information about the potential toxic effects of the drug candidate when administered for a longer duration.

Chronic toxicity studies are conducted to assess the potential toxicological effects of the drug candidate when administered over a prolonged period of time. These studies typically last for 6 to 12 months and involve daily dosing of the animals. The animals are observed for changes in body weight, organ function, and any signs of toxicity. Chronic toxicity studies provide important information about the potential long-term toxic effects of the drug candidate.

Carcinogenicity studies are conducted to evaluate the potential of the drug candidate to cause cancer. These studies typically last for 2 years and involve daily dosing of the animals. The animals are observed for the development of tumors and any signs of toxicity. Carcinogenicity studies provide important information about the potential carcinogenic effects of the drug candidate.

Reproductive and developmental toxicity studies are conducted to evaluate the potential effects of the drug candidate on fertility, embryonic development, and postnatal development. These studies are typically conducted in two generations of animals and involve daily dosing of the animals. The animals are observed for changes in reproductive function and any signs of toxicity. Reproductive and developmental toxicity studies provide important information about the potential effects of the drug candidate on reproductive and developmental health.

Immunotoxicity studies are conducted to evaluate the potential effects of the drug candidate on the immune system. These studies involve daily dosing of the animals and the assessment of immune function. The animals are observed for any changes in immune function and any signs of toxicity. Immunotoxicity studies provide important information about the potential effects of the drug candidate on the immune system.

Genotoxicity studies are conducted to evaluate the potential of the drug candidate to cause mutations in genetic material. These studies typically involve the use of in vitro and in vivo assays to assess the potential genotoxic effects of the drug candidate. Genotoxicity studies provide important information about the potential mutagenic effects of the drug candidate.

17.4 Safety Data Generation in Clinical Phase

The clinical phase of drug development is the stage of research that involves testing a drug candidate in human subjects. This phase typically follows pre-clinical studies that evaluate a drug candidate's safety and efficacy in non-human subjects such as animals. The clinical phase consists of three stages, namely Phase I, Phase II, and Phase III clinical trials.

Importance of safety data generation in Clinical Phase

The primary objective of clinical trials is to evaluate the safety and efficacy of a drug candidate in humans. Therefore, safety data generation is a crucial component of clinical trials to ensure that potential toxic effects are identified and appropriately managed. This information is critical in the decision-making process for regulatory agencies, healthcare providers, and patients.

Clinical trials involve testing a drug candidate's safety and efficacy in a diverse patient population. Therefore, it is essential to generate safety data that is representative of the targeted patient population, including vulnerable groups such as elderly, pediatric, and pregnant patients. Safety data generation in clinical trials can help identify any potential adverse effects associated with the drug candidate and provide valuable information on appropriate dosing, drug interactions, and patient management.

Examples of the importance of safety data generation in clinical trials can be seen in the history of drug development. For instance, the drug thalidomide was initially marketed as a sedative and anti-nausea medication. However, during the 1950s and 1960s, it was discovered that thalidomide caused severe birth defects when taken by pregnant women. The adverse effects of thalidomide led to the development of strict regulations on drug development and the establishment of clinical trial guidelines to ensure patient safety.

In addition, safety data generation in clinical trials is essential in the development of new therapies for conditions that lack effective treatment options. For example, the recent approval of mRNA vaccines for COVID-19 is a significant milestone in drug development. The safety data generated during clinical trials played a crucial role in the rapid approval and widespread distribution of these vaccines.

17.5 Types of Clinical Studies for Safety Data Generation

17.5.1 Phase 1 Clinical Trials

Phase 1 clinical trials are the first step in evaluating the safety and tolerability of a new drug candidate in humans. These trials are typically conducted in a small number of healthy volunteers, with the primary objective of assessing the drug's safety profile and pharmacokinetics. During phase 1 trials, the drug candidate is administered at a low dose, and the dose is gradually increased to determine the highest dose that can be safely administered without causing significant adverse effects.

Phase 1 trials are critical for identifying any potential safety concerns early in the drug development process, before larger and more expensive trials are conducted. In addition to evaluating the safety profile of a drug candidate, phase 1 trials can also provide valuable information on the drug's pharmacokinetic properties, such as absorption, distribution, metabolism, and excretion. This information is important for determining the appropriate dosing regimen for future clinical trials.

For example, a phase 1 clinical trial of a new cancer drug may involve healthy volunteers who are given increasing doses of the drug over a period of several weeks. During the trial, the researchers would monitor the volunteers for any adverse effects, such as nausea, vomiting, or changes in blood pressure. They would also collect blood samples to measure the drug's concentration in the body and determine its pharmacokinetic properties. Based on the results of the phase 1 trial, the researchers would be able to determine the highest safe dose of the drug for future trials and assess its potential efficacy in treating cancer.

17.5.2 Phase 2 Clinical Trials

Phase 2 clinical trials are the second stage of clinical studies in drug development and aim to determine the safety and effectiveness of the drug candidate in a larger population of patients. The primary objective of phase 2 trials is to gather preliminary evidence of the drug's effectiveness in treating the target disease or condition and to further evaluate its safety.

Phase 2 clinical trials typically involve a few hundred patients who have the target disease or condition, and they are usually randomized, controlled studies. In some cases, phase 2 trials may be non-randomized and uncontrolled if the drug candidate is being studied for rare diseases or conditions with few available treatment options.

During phase 2 clinical trials, researchers collect safety data by monitoring adverse events, laboratory tests, and vital signs. The data is then analyzed to assess the safety and tolerability of the drug candidate, as well as to identify any potential adverse effects.

If the phase 2 trial is successful, the drug candidate may proceed to phase 3 clinical trials. However, if safety concerns arise during the phase 2 trial, the drug candidate may be discontinued or modified before moving on to the next phase of clinical development.

An example of a successful phase 2 clinical trial is the use of the drug Imatinib in the treatment of chronic myelogenous leukemia (CML). In a phase 2 trial, Imatinib was found to be highly effective in treating CML, leading to its approval by regulatory agencies for the treatment of the disease.

17.5.3 Phase 3 Clinical Trials

Phase 3 clinical trials are conducted after the successful completion of Phase 2 studies and are designed to evaluate the efficacy and safety of the investigational drug in a larger population. These trials typically involve hundreds to thousands of participants and are randomized, double-blind, and placebo-controlled.

The primary objective of Phase 3 trials is to establish the safety and efficacy of the investigational drug in a diverse patient population, including those with comorbidities and patients taking other medications. Phase 3 studies can also be used to identify rare adverse events that may not have been detected during earlier phases of clinical development due to the smaller sample size.

In addition to safety and efficacy, Phase 3 trials may also evaluate the optimal dose and duration of treatment, as well as the drug's effectiveness in specific patient subgroups. Phase 3 studies may also include long-term follow-up to assess the drug's safety and efficacy over extended periods.

Phase 3 clinical trials play a critical role in providing the data necessary for regulatory authorities to make informed decisions about the approval of a new drug. The results of these studies are used to support the submission of a New Drug Application (NDA) to regulatory agencies such as the U.S. Food and Drug Administration (FDA) and the European Medicines Agency (EMA). If the drug is approved, the data from Phase 3 trials also inform the drug's labeling and prescribing information, which provides important safety information for healthcare providers and patients.

17.5.4 Phase 4 clinical trials

Phase 4 clinical trials, also known as post-marketing surveillance trials, are conducted after a drug has been approved and is available on the market. These trials are designed to collect additional safety and efficacy data in larger populations over a longer period of time. The main objectives of phase 4 trials are to identify rare adverse reactions, evaluate long-term safety and effectiveness, and explore new indications or uses for the drug.

Phase 4 trials are usually initiated by pharmaceutical companies, but they may also be required by regulatory agencies as a condition for drug approval or to address safety concerns that arise after the drug is on the market. These trials often involve large numbers of patients and can be conducted over several years.

One example of a phase 4 trial is the Post-Marketing Anticoagulation Reversal Treatment Evaluation Study (PACTE), which evaluated the effectiveness and safety of four different agents for reversing anticoagulation in patients with major bleeding. The trial included over 1,500 patients across 168 sites and was conducted over a period of four years.

Another example is the Observational Study of Influenza Vaccine in the Elderly (OSIVE), which evaluated the safety and effectiveness of an influenza vaccine in elderly patients. The trial included over 25,000 patients and was conducted over four flu seasons.

Phase 4 trials play an important role in monitoring the safety and effectiveness of drugs after they are approved and on the market. They provide valuable information to healthcare providers and patients, and can inform regulatory decisions regarding the use of the drug.

17.6 Safety Data Generation in Clinical Studies

17. 6.1 Adverse Event Monitoring and Reporting

Adverse Event (AE) monitoring and reporting is a critical component of safety data generation in clinical studies. AE refers to any undesirable medical occurrence in a patient who has received a drug or a placebo. AE can be classified as mild, moderate, or severe depending on the severity of the symptoms and the impact on the patient's health. AE monitoring involves the systematic collection and evaluation of AE data during clinical studies to identify and report any safety concerns associated with the drug under investigation.

AE monitoring starts during the Phase 1 clinical trial and continues throughout the entire drug development process. During clinical studies, investigators are required to report all AEs to the study sponsor, who is responsible for collecting and analyzing the data. The study sponsor is required to report serious and unexpected AEs to regulatory agencies such as the FDA or EMA within a specified timeframe.

In addition to AE monitoring, safety data can also be generated through other methods such as laboratory tests, imaging studies, and vital signs monitoring. For example, laboratory tests can be used to monitor liver and kidney function, while imaging studies such as MRI or CT scans can be used to detect structural changes in organs.

Overall, AE monitoring and reporting is a critical component of safety data generation in clinical studies. It enables the identification of potential safety concerns associated with a drug candidate, which can inform decision-making throughout the drug development process.

17.6.2. laboratory testing

In addition to adverse event monitoring and reporting, laboratory testing is also an essential component of safety data generation in clinical studies. Laboratory tests can help to identify potential safety concerns related to a drug candidate by assessing its effects on various physiological parameters.

The types of laboratory tests used in clinical studies can vary depending on the specific drug candidate and its proposed indication. Common laboratory tests include blood chemistry tests, hematology tests, and urinalysis. These tests can provide information on potential adverse effects of a drug candidate on organ function, such as liver or kidney toxicity.

For example, in a clinical trial evaluating a new diabetes medication, laboratory tests may be used to monitor changes in blood glucose levels, kidney function, and liver function. Any abnormalities identified in these laboratory tests can indicate potential safety concerns related to the drug candidate.

It is important for clinical trials to have standardized laboratory procedures to ensure consistent and reliable data. This includes the use of validated laboratory assays, standardized sample collection and handling procedures, and trained laboratory personnel. Any deviations from standard laboratory procedures can lead to unreliable or inaccurate safety data.

Overall, laboratory testing is an important tool for safety data generation in clinical studies and should be carefully designed and executed to ensure accurate and reliable results.

17.6.3 ECG Monitoring

ECG monitoring is another method used for safety data generation in clinical studies. Electrocardiography (ECG) measures the electrical activity of the heart and can provide valuable information on drug-induced changes in cardiac function. ECG monitoring is often included in clinical trials, particularly those involving drugs that may affect cardiac function.

For example, a clinical trial of a new antiarrhythmic drug may include ECG monitoring to assess its effect on cardiac function. The trial may involve monitoring ECG at baseline, during treatment, and after treatment to assess changes in cardiac function over time. Any abnormalities observed in ECG may be reported as adverse events, and the data may be used to determine the safety profile of the drug.

ECG monitoring is an important tool for safety data generation in clinical studies as it can detect cardiac effects that may not be apparent based on clinical symptoms alone. It can also be used to identify patients who may be at increased risk for cardiac events and to monitor the cardiac safety of drugs already on the market.

In addition to adverse event monitoring and reporting, laboratory testing is also an essential component of safety data generation in clinical studies. Laboratory tests can help to identify potential safety concerns related to a drug candidate by assessing its effects on various physiological parameters.

The types of laboratory tests used in clinical studies can vary depending on the specific drug candidate and its proposed indication. Common laboratory tests include blood chemistry tests, hematology tests, and urinalysis. These tests can provide information on potential adverse effects of a drug candidate on organ function, such as liver or kidney toxicity.

For example, in a clinical trial evaluating a new diabetes medication, laboratory tests may be used to monitor changes in blood glucose levels, kidney function, and liver function. Any abnormalities identified in these laboratory tests can indicate potential safety concerns related to the drug candidate.

It is important for clinical trials to have standardized laboratory procedures to ensure consistent and reliable data. This includes the use of validated laboratory assays, standardized sample collection and handling procedures, and trained laboratory personnel. Any deviations from standard laboratory procedures can lead to unreliable or inaccurate safety data.

Overall, laboratory testing is an important tool for safety data generation in clinical studies and should be carefully designed and executed to ensure accurate and reliable results.

17.6.4 Imaging Studies

Imaging studies are another tool for safety data generation in clinical studies. They can be used to identify potential drug-related changes in anatomy, physiology, or function. Imaging studies are commonly used to evaluate the safety of drugs targeting the central nervous system, such as those used for the treatment of Alzheimer's disease or multiple sclerosis.

Different types of imaging studies can be used depending on the drug's mechanism of action and potential safety concerns. For example, magnetic resonance imaging (MRI) is often used to evaluate the safety of drugs that may affect brain structure or function. Positron emission tomography (PET) scans can be used to study metabolic changes in tissues, while computed tomography (CT) scans can be used to evaluate changes in bone density or structure.

In addition to providing safety data, imaging studies can also provide information on drug efficacy. For example, changes in tumor size can be monitored using imaging studies in oncology trials.

However, imaging studies can be costly and may not be feasible for all clinical studies. Moreover, the interpretation of imaging studies requires specialized expertise, and inter-reader variability can affect the reliability of results. Therefore, imaging studies should be used judiciously and in conjunction with other safety monitoring methods in clinical studies.

17.6.5 Biomarker Studies

Biomarkers are measurable indicators that can be used to evaluate various biological processes, including disease development and response to treatment. Biomarker studies are an important aspect of safety data generation in clinical studies. By analyzing biomarkers, researchers can gain insight into the potential safety and efficacy of a drug candidate.

Biomarkers can be used to identify patients who are at higher risk for adverse effects, to monitor the progression of disease, and to assess the impact of treatment. For example, in a clinical trial for a cancer drug, researchers may measure tumor biomarkers to evaluate the drug's effectiveness in shrinking tumors and preventing their growth. Biomarkers can also be used to identify potential adverse effects before they become clinically apparent. For instance, elevated liver enzymes may indicate liver toxicity before clinical symptoms appear.

In addition to identifying potential safety concerns, biomarker studies can also help to identify patient subgroups that may benefit more from the drug. For example, in a clinical trial for a diabetes drug, researchers may use biomarkers to identify patients who have a specific genetic mutation that makes them more likely to respond to the drug.

Biomarkers can be measured through various techniques, including blood tests, imaging studies, and genetic testing. It is important to use validated biomarkers and standardized techniques to ensure that the results are accurate and reliable. Regulatory agencies such as the FDA and EMA may require biomarker studies as part of the safety data generation in clinical studies.

17.7 Safety data generation in Post approval Phase

The post-approval phase in drug development refers to the stage after a drug has been approved by regulatory authorities and made available for use by patients. During this phase, additional safety data is generated to monitor and evaluate the long-term safety and effectiveness of the drug in real-world settings.

17.7.1 Importance of safety data generation in post-approval phase

While pre-clinical and clinical studies provide valuable safety data, they are often limited in terms of sample size and duration of exposure. The post-approval phase allows for the collection of safety data in larger, more diverse patient populations over longer periods of time. This data is critical for detecting rare or delayed adverse events, identifying patient subpopulations that may be at increased risk, and informing decisions regarding the safe use of the drug.

17.7.2 Types of Post-Approval Studies for Safety Data Generation

A. Phase 4 Clinical Trials

Phase 4 clinical trials are studies that are conducted after a drug has been approved and marketed. They are designed to assess the long-term safety and effectiveness of the drug in real-world settings. Phase 4 studies may involve larger patient populations and longer follow-up periods than previous phases of clinical development. They may also evaluate additional patient outcomes beyond those assessed in earlier phases, such as quality of life and economic impact.

B. Post-Marketing Surveillance Studies

Post-marketing surveillance studies are non-interventional studies that are conducted to monitor the safety and effectiveness of a drug after it has been approved and marketed. These studies may involve the collection of safety data from large populations of patients or from specific patient subpopulations. They may also involve the comparison of safety data between different drugs or different formulations of the same drug.

C. Patient Registries

Patient registries are databases that collect data on patients with a specific condition or who are receiving a particular treatment. Registries can be used to monitor the long-term safety and effectiveness of drugs in real-world settings. They may also be used to identify patient subpopulations that may be at increased risk of adverse events.

D. Meta-Analyses and Systematic Reviews

Meta-analyses and systematic reviews are methods for combining data from multiple studies to generate a comprehensive summary of the available evidence. These methods can be used to evaluate the safety and effectiveness of drugs in real-world settings, as well as to identify potential safety concerns.

17.8 Safety Data Generation in Post-Approval Studies

A. Adverse Event Monitoring and Reporting

Adverse event monitoring and reporting is a critical component of safety data generation in post-approval studies. Adverse events may be reported through spontaneous reporting systems, such as the FDA Adverse Event Reporting System (FAERS), or through active surveillance methods, such as medical record review or patient surveys. Adverse events may also be detected through data mining techniques, such as signal detection methods.

B. Laboratory Testing

Laboratory testing may be used to monitor the safety and effectiveness of drugs in real-world settings. For example, laboratory testing may be used to monitor liver function in patients receiving a hepatotoxic drug, or to monitor kidney function in patients receiving a nephrotoxic drug.

C. Biomarker Studies

Biomarker studies may be used to identify patient subpopulations that may be at increased risk of adverse events, or to monitor the effectiveness of a drug in real-world settings. For example, biomarker studies may be used to monitor changes in blood pressure or cholesterol levels in patients receiving a cardiovascular drug.

D. Health Outcomes Research

Health outcomes research is a field of study that focuses on evaluating the impact of healthcare interventions on patient outcomes, such as mortality, morbidity, and quality of life. Health outcomes research may be used to evaluate the long-term safety and

effectiveness of drugs in real-world settings, which is important for generating safety data during the post-approval phase. Health outcomes research can involve observational studies or randomized controlled trials, and may use a variety of data sources such as electronic health records, administrative claims data, or patient-reported outcomes.

One example of health outcomes research in post-approval safety data generation is the use of comparative effectiveness research to evaluate the safety and effectiveness of different treatment options for a specific condition. This type of research may involve comparing the safety profiles of drugs with similar indications, or evaluating the safety of a new drug compared to standard of care treatments. By evaluating safety outcomes over a longer period of time and in a larger and more diverse patient population, health outcomes research can provide valuable information on the real-world safety profile of a drug.

Another example of health outcomes research is the use of pharmacoepidemiology studies to evaluate the safety of drugs in specific patient populations. These studies may focus on vulnerable populations such as pregnant women, children, or the elderly, and can provide important safety data that may not have been captured during pre-approval clinical trials. For example, a pharmacoepidemiology study may evaluate the risk of birth defects associated with a specific drug during pregnancy.

17.9 Statistical Methods for Evaluating Medication Safety Data

17.9.1 Signal detection methods

This method involves using data mining techniques to identify patterns of adverse events that may be associated with a particular drug. Signal detection can be used to identify potential safety concerns even when the frequency of the adverse events is not high enough to trigger a disproportionality analysis.

Signal detection methods are commonly used in pharmacovigilance to detect safety signals from large databases of adverse event reports. These methods are designed to identify potential safety concerns by comparing the frequency of a particular adverse event in association with a given drug to the expected frequency of that event in the absence of drug exposure. There are several statistical methods for signal detection, including proportional reporting ratio (PRR), reporting odds ratio (ROR), information component (IC), empirical Bayes geometric mean (EBGM), and Bayesian Confidence Propagation Neural Network (BCPNN).

A. Proportional reporting ratio (PRR)

PRR is a simple method for detecting safety signals that compares the proportion of reports for a given drug and adverse event combination to the proportion of reports for the same adverse event across all drugs in the database. A high PRR indicates that the drug is associated with a higher than expected frequency of the adverse event.

B. Reporting odds ratio (ROR)

ROR is a variation of PRR that calculates the odds of a particular adverse event being reported for a given drug compared to all other drugs in the database. A high ROR indicates a higher than expected association between the drug and the adverse event.

C. Information component (IC)

IC is a Bayesian method that uses prior information on the association between drugs and adverse events to calculate the strength of association between a drug and a specific adverse event. IC values greater than zero indicate a positive association between the drug and the adverse event, while values less than zero indicate a negative association.

D. Empirical Bayes geometric mean (EBGM)

EBGM is a modification of IC that takes into account the variability of reporting rates for both the drug and the adverse event. The method calculates the ratio of observed to expected reports for a given drug and adverse event combination, with a value greater than one indicating a potential safety signal.

E. Bayesian Confidence Propagation Neural Network (BCPNN)

BCPNN is a machine learning method that uses Bayesian inference to model the association between a drug and a specific adverse event. The method incorporates prior knowledge of the drug's safety profile and adapts to new data as it becomes available, allowing for real-time monitoring of drug safety.

17.9.2 Descriptive methods

Descriptive methods are commonly used to summarize and describe medication safety data in terms of adverse event frequency, duration, and severity.

Adverse event frequency: This method involves counting the number of occurrences of a particular adverse event over a specific period of time or in a specific population. This information can be presented in the form of a frequency distribution, which can provide insight into the prevalence of adverse events associated with a particular medication.

Adverse event duration: This method involves describing the duration of adverse events associated with a particular medication. The duration of an adverse event can be defined as the length of time from the onset of the event to its resolution or the time at which the event is no longer considered to be clinically significant. Describing the duration of adverse events can help to identify trends or patterns in the occurrence of adverse events and can inform decisions about the management of these events.

Adverse event severity: This method involves categorizing the severity of adverse events associated with a particular medication. Severity can be defined in a number of ways, including the impact of the event on the patient's daily life, the level of medical intervention required to manage the event, and the potential for the event to result in long-term harm. Categorizing adverse events by severity can help to identify events that are particularly concerning and may require additional attention in terms of risk management or regulatory action.

17.9.3 Inferential methods

A. Case-control studies

Inferential methods, such as case-control studies, aim to identify risk factors for adverse events associated with medications. In case-control studies, a group of patients who have experienced the adverse event (cases) are compared with a group of patients who have not experienced the adverse event (controls) to determine if there is an association between the medication and the adverse event. The analysis typically involves calculating the odds ratio (OR) of exposure to the medication in cases compared to controls. If the OR is significantly greater than 1, this suggests a positive association between the medication and the adverse event.

One example of a case-control study in medication safety is the investigation of the association between selective serotonin reuptake inhibitors (SSRIs) and the risk of suicide attempts in young adults. In this study, a group of patients who attempted suicide while taking SSRIs were compared to a group of patients who attempted suicide but were not taking SSRIs. The analysis found that the odds of SSRI use were significantly higher in the group of patients who attempted suicide while taking SSRIs, suggesting a positive association between SSRI use and the risk of suicide attempts in young adults.

B. Cohort studies

Cohort studies are another type of inferential method used in evaluating medication safety data. In a cohort study, a group of individuals who have been exposed to a medication are followed over time and compared to a group of individuals who have not been exposed to the medication. The two groups are then compared for the occurrence of adverse events. Cohort studies can be either prospective or retrospective.

Prospective cohort studies involve following a group of individuals who have been exposed to a medication over a period of time and monitoring them for the occurrence of adverse events. Retrospective cohort studies, on the other hand, involve identifying a group of individuals who have been exposed to a medication in the past and comparing them to a group of individuals who have not been exposed to the medication.

Cohort studies are useful in evaluating medication safety data as they allow for the identification of potential adverse events associated with medication use in a large group of patients over an extended period of time. They also allow for the estimation of the incidence and prevalence of adverse events, as well as the identification of risk factors associated with adverse events. However, cohort studies can be time-consuming and costly to conduct and may require a large sample size to ensure statistical power.

C. Randomized controlled trials (RCTs)

Randomized controlled trials (RCTs) are a type of inferential statistical method used to evaluate medication safety data. RCTs are experimental studies where participants are randomly assigned to either a treatment group or a control group. The treatment group receives the medication being studied, while the control group receives a placebo or standard treatment.

RCTs are typically designed to evaluate the efficacy of a medication, but they can also be used to evaluate safety outcomes. Adverse events and other safety data are collected during the trial and compared between the treatment and control groups. Statistical methods such as chi-square tests, t-tests, and logistic regression are often used to analyze the safety data collected in RCTs.

RCTs are considered to be the gold standard for evaluating medication safety because they are designed to minimize bias and confounding variables. However, they can be expensive and time-consuming to conduct, and may not always be feasible for studying rare adverse events or long-term safety outcomes.

17.9.4 Regression analysis

Regression analysis is a statistical method that is commonly used in pharmacovigilance to evaluate the relationship between a drug and a specific adverse event. It is an essential tool for identifying and quantifying the risks associated with medications. The method involves examining a large set of data that includes information on the drug in question, the adverse event, and any potential confounding variables that may affect the relationship between the drug and the adverse event.

Regression analysis allows researchers to control for other factors that may influence the occurrence of an adverse event. These factors can include patient demographics, co-morbidities, concomitant medications, and other relevant clinical information. By controlling for these variables, researchers can better assess the relationship between a drug and an adverse event, and determine whether the relationship is causal or not.

There are several types of regression analysis used in pharmacovigilance, including logistic regression, Poisson regression, and Cox proportional hazards regression. Logistic regression is commonly used to evaluate the relationship between a binary outcome (such as the presence or absence of an adverse event) and one or more predictor variables (such as a drug or a patient characteristic). Poisson regression is used to model count data, such as the number of adverse events reported for a specific drug. Cox proportional hazards regression is used to model time-to-event data, such as the time from drug initiation to the occurrence of an adverse event.

Regression analysis is a powerful tool for pharmacovigilance because it can identify risk factors associated with specific adverse events. This information can be used to develop strategies to minimize the risks associated with medication use. Additionally, regression analysis can help to identify patient populations that may be at increased risk for specific adverse events, allowing for targeted monitoring and interventions. Overall, regression analysis is an essential component of pharmacovigilance that plays a critical role in ensuring medication safety.

17.9.5 Bayesian methods

Bayesian methods are a class of statistical methods that involve updating prior probabilities with new data or information. In pharmacovigilance, Bayesian methods can be used to estimate the probability of an adverse event occurring given a patient's demographic and clinical characteristics. This is particularly useful when dealing with rare events or when the available data is limited.

Bayesian methods can also be used to calculate the probability that a specific drug is causing an adverse event, known as the Bayesian Credibility Interval. This interval provides a range of probabilities within which the true causal relationship between the drug and the adverse event is likely to lie. Bayesian methods can also be used in signal detection and risk management, allowing for the updating of probabilities as new data becomes available.

Overall, Bayesian methods are a powerful tool in pharmacovigilance, allowing for the estimation of probabilities and the updating of prior beliefs based on new information. They can help to identify potential safety issues with drugs and facilitate decision-making in risk management.

There are several different Bayesian methods used in pharmacovigilance, including:

Bayesian hierarchical models: This approach allows for the estimation of drug safety profiles at different levels, such as individual patients, specific populations, and overall populations.

Bayesian network analysis: This method uses a graphical model to represent the relationships between different variables, including drug exposure and adverse events.

Bayesian logistic regression: This method estimates the probability of an adverse event occurring given a patient's exposure to a particular drug, taking into account other patient-specific variables.

Bayesian signal detection: This method combines different sources of data, such as spontaneous reports and electronic health records, to detect signals of potential adverse drug reactions.

17.9.6 Disproportionality analysis.

Disproportionality analysis is a statistical method used in pharmacovigilance to identify potential safety signals or associations between a drug and an adverse event. This method is based on the concept of disproportionality, which is the extent to which an adverse event is reported for a particular drug compared to what would be expected based on its frequency in the general population.

Disproportionality analysis typically involves the use of a spontaneous reporting database, such as the FDA Adverse Event Reporting System (FAERS) or the European Medicines Agency's EudraVigilance database, which contains reports of adverse events associated with drugs. The analysis compares the frequency of a particular adverse event in relation to the frequency of the drug being used.Disproportionality analysis is a useful tool in pharmacovigilance as it can help identify potential safety signals, which can then be investigated further through additional studies or monitoring. However, it is important to note that disproportionality analysis does not provide definitive evidence of causality and should be used in conjunction with other methods to assess drug safety.

17.9.7 Diference between disproportionality analysis and signal detection methods

Adverse event disproportionality analysis and signal detection methods are two related but distinct approaches used in pharmacovigilance to identify potential safety signals.

Disproportionality analysis involves comparing the observed frequency of a particular adverse event with the expected frequency based on the known use of a drug in a given population. If the observed frequency is higher than the expected frequency, it suggests a potential safety signal for further investigation.

Signal detection methods, on the other hand, involve a more comprehensive analysis of safety data using various statistical techniques. These methods not only identify potential safety signals based on disproportionality analysis but also take into account other factors such as the severity and novelty of the adverse event, the time between drug exposure and the event, and the strength of the association between the drug and the event.

XVIII

Guidelines for Pharmacovigilance

The International Conference on Harmonisation of Technical Requirements for Registration of Pharmaceuticals for Human Use (ICH) has developed guidelines for the conduct of pharmacovigilance studies and reporting of adverse drug reactions (ADRs). These guidelines aim to harmonize the pharmacovigilance practices across different regions of the world and to ensure the safety of patients using pharmaceutical products. The guidelines provide recommendations for various aspects of pharmacovigilance, including signal detection, management of risks, and reporting of ADRs. Adherence to these guidelines is often a regulatory requirement for drug manufacturers, making them an essential component of the pharmacovigilance system. In this unit, we will discuss the key ICH guidelines related to pharmacovigilance and their implications for the industry and regulatory authorities.

18.1 Organization and objectives of ICH

The International Council for Harmonisation of Technical Requirements for Pharmaceuticals for Human Use (ICH) is a global organization that brings together regulatory authorities and the pharmaceutical industry to develop and promote harmonized guidelines for the development, registration, and post-approval safety monitoring of pharmaceutical products. The ICH was established in 1990 and currently has members from Europe, Japan, the United States, Canada, and other countries.

The objectives of the ICH are to improve the efficiency of drug development and regulatory approval, promote safety and effectiveness of pharmaceutical products, and facilitate global trade of pharmaceuticals. To achieve these objectives, the ICH has developed a series of guidelines that provide recommendations and standards for various aspects of drug development and post-approval safety monitoring.

The ICH guidelines are voluntary and not legally binding, but they are widely accepted and implemented by regulatory authorities and the pharmaceutical industry worldwide. The guidelines are regularly reviewed and updated to reflect advances in scientific knowledge, changes in regulatory requirements, and emerging safety concerns.

The ICH guidelines cover a wide range of topics, including quality, safety, and efficacy of pharmaceutical products, clinical trial design, data management and analysis, and pharmacovigilance. The guidelines related to pharmacovigilance provide recommendations for the collection, management, and reporting of adverse drug reactions (ADRs), signal detection, risk management, and communication between regulatory authorities and the pharmaceutical industry.

The ICH guidelines for pharmacovigilance include the ICH E2A guideline on the clinical safety data management, the ICH E2B guideline on the electronic transmission of individual case safety reports (ICSRs), the ICH E2C guideline on periodic safety update reports (PSURs), the ICH E2D guideline on the post-approval safety data management, the ICH E2E guideline on pharmacovigilance planning, the ICH E2F guideline on development safety update reports (DSURs), and the ICH E6(R2) guideline on good clinical practice.

18.2 Expedited reporting

Expedited reporting is a vital component of pharmacovigilance that facilitates the timely identification and management of adverse drug reactions (ADRs). It is a regulatory requirement that marketing authorization holders (MAHs) report serious and unexpected ADRs to the regulatory authorities within a specific timeframe.

The International Council for Harmonisation of Technical Requirements for Pharmaceuticals for Human Use (ICH) has provided guidelines on expedited reporting, which have been adopted by regulatory authorities worldwide. These guidelines provide a framework for MAHs to comply with expedited reporting requirements, with a focus on ensuring patient safety.

The ICH guidelines outline the criteria for determining which adverse reactions are considered serious and unexpected, and therefore subject to expedited reporting. The criteria include events that are fatal, life-threatening, require hospitalization, result in disability or permanent damage, or are congenital anomalies. The guidelines also define what constitutes an unexpected ADR, which includes reactions not listed in the product information or occurring at a higher frequency or severity than expected.

The guidelines further specify the time frame for reporting serious and unexpected ADRs, which is typically within 15 calendar days of the receipt of the information by the MAH. The reporting timeframe may be shorter in some cases, such as for fatal or life-threatening reactions, which must be reported immediately upon receipt of the information.

MAHs are also required to submit periodic safety update reports (PSURs) to the regulatory authorities, which include a summary of all adverse reactions that have occurred since the last report. PSURs are typically submitted at regular intervals, which vary depending on the stage of drug development and approval.

The ICH guidelines emphasize the importance of quality management systems in ensuring the accuracy and completeness of expedited reporting. MAHs are required to establish procedures for the timely detection, assessment, and reporting of ADRs, as well as for monitoring the safety profile of their products.

18.3 Individual case safety reports

The Individual Case Safety Report (ICSR) is a crucial component of pharmacovigilance. It is the primary means by which adverse drug reactions (ADRs) are reported to regulatory authorities around the world. An ICSR is a record of a single patient's experience with a particular drug or medical product that resulted in an adverse event. It is an important tool for identifying safety signals and trends related to drug use.

ICSRs contain information on the patient, the drug or product, and the adverse event. The information typically includes demographic data such as age and sex, medical history, details about the drug such as dose and frequency of use, and a description of the adverse event, including the time of onset and the outcome. The information may also include concomitant medications, laboratory values, and any relevant medical tests.

The ICSR is an important tool for tracking the safety of drugs and medical products. Regulatory authorities require that pharmaceutical companies and healthcare providers report any serious adverse events associated with their products to the appropriate regulatory authority. ICSRs are used to identify safety signals and trends, and to monitor the safety of drugs and medical products over time.

There are several challenges associated with the collection and reporting of ICSRs. One of the challenges is the variability in the quality and completeness of the information reported. This can be due to a lack of knowledge or awareness about the importance of reporting ADRs, or to the fact that the reporting process can be time-consuming and cumbersome. Another challenge is the need to reconcile different terminologies used by different countries and organizations, which can result in inconsistent or incomplete reporting.

To address these challenges, regulatory authorities have established guidelines for the reporting of ICSRs. The International

Council for Harmonisation of Technical Requirements for Pharmaceuticals for Human Use (ICH) has published guidelines for the reporting of ICSRs, including guidelines for the format and content of ICSRs, and guidelines for expedited reporting of serious adverse events.

The guidelines provide a standardized approach to reporting adverse events, which helps to ensure that the information collected is consistent and complete. They also help to ensure that ICSRs are submitted in a timely manner and that serious adverse events are reported as soon as possible.

18.4 *Periodic safety update reports*

The International Council for Harmonisation of Technical Requirements for Pharmaceuticals for Human Use (ICH) provides guidelines for the pharmaceutical industry regarding drug development, registration, and post-marketing surveillance. One important aspect of post-marketing surveillance is the periodic safety update report (PSUR).

A PSUR is a comprehensive document that evaluates the safety profile of a drug product over a defined period of time. It includes an analysis of data from various sources, such as spontaneous reports, clinical trials, epidemiological studies, and other sources of safety data. The primary objective of a PSUR is to identify any new safety concerns or trends in the use of the drug product, and to determine whether any changes in the product's benefit-risk balance are necessary.

The content and frequency of PSURs are determined by regulatory authorities based on the characteristics of the drug product, the nature and extent of its use, and the level of safety concerns associated with the product. Typically, PSURs are submitted annually for the first three to five years after a drug product is approved, and then every two to three years thereafter, depending on the risk-benefit profile of the product.

The ICH has developed guidelines on the format and content of PSURs, known as the ICH E2C guideline. The guideline specifies the core data elements that should be included in a PSUR, such as the drug's pharmacovigilance history, clinical safety data, epidemiological data, and a summary of any safety concerns or changes in the product's benefit-risk balance.

In addition to the core data elements, the ICH E2C guideline also provides recommendations on the presentation of the data, the use of statistical methods to identify safety signals, and the reporting of safety concerns to regulatory authorities. The guideline also includes requirements for the preparation, submission, and review of PSURs by regulatory authorities.

PSURs are an important tool for monitoring the safety of drug products in the post-marketing period. The ICH E2C guideline provides a framework for the preparation and submission of PSURs, and helps ensure that the safety of drug products is monitored in a consistent and comprehensive manner across regulatory authorities.

18.5 Post approval expedited reporting

Post-approval expedited reporting is a key component of pharmacovigilance, aimed at ensuring the continued safety of medicinal products even after they have been approved and marketed. The International Council for Harmonisation (ICH) has established guidelines and regulations to standardize post-approval expedited reporting practices.

The primary objective of post-approval expedited reporting is to identify and report adverse drug reactions (ADRs) that were not previously identified during clinical trials or that were not observed frequently enough to warrant regulatory action. This is important for ensuring that drugs remain safe for their intended use, and for minimizing the risks of unexpected side effects or adverse events.

Post-approval expedited reporting is typically triggered by the receipt of new safety information or by a change in the risk-benefit profile of a medicinal product. Regulatory authorities may require marketing authorization holders to submit a post-approval expedited report within a specific timeframe, depending on the severity of the safety concern and the level of risk to public health.

The ICH guidelines for post-approval expedited reporting provide specific requirements for the content and format of such reports. In general, these reports should contain information about the suspected adverse reaction, the product(s) involved, the patient(s) affected, the outcome(s), and any relevant laboratory data or other clinical information.

In addition to providing guidance on the contents of post-approval expedited reports, the ICH guidelines also outline the process for submitting such reports to regulatory authorities. This includes requirements for electronic submission, timelines for reporting, and procedures for follow-up and communication between regulatory authorities and marketing authorization holders.

Post-approval expedited reporting is a critical aspect of pharmacovigilance, as it helps to ensure that drugs remain safe and effective for their intended use. The ICH guidelines provide a framework for ensuring that the reporting of adverse events is timely, accurate, and standardized, which helps to improve patient safety and public health.

18.6 Pharmacovigilance planning

Pharmacovigilance planning refers to the process of developing a comprehensive plan to monitor and evaluate the safety and efficacy of medicinal products. It is an essential component of drug development and regulatory approval processes, and helps to ensure the continued safety and effectiveness of drugs once they are on the market.

The planning process typically involves the establishment of a pharmacovigilance system that outlines the roles and responsibilities of various stakeholders, including drug manufacturers, regulatory agencies, healthcare professionals, and patients. The system should also include procedures for the collection, evaluation, and dissemination of safety information, as well as methods for risk management and communication.

One of the key elements of pharmacovigilance planning is the development of a risk management plan (RMP), which outlines the potential risks associated with a drug and how they will be monitored and managed throughout its lifecycle. The RMP should include measures for early detection and response to safety issues, as well as plans for communication with stakeholders.

Another important aspect of pharmacovigilance planning is the establishment of post-marketing surveillance systems, such as spontaneous reporting systems, active surveillance programs, and clinical trials. These systems help to identify potential safety issues that may not have been detected during pre-market clinical trials, and provide ongoing monitoring of drug safety throughout its lifecycle.

In addition to establishing pharmacovigilance systems and risk management plans, effective pharmacovigilance planning requires the development of training programs for healthcare professionals, patients, and other stakeholders. These programs should provide education on drug safety issues and adverse event reporting, and help to promote a culture of safety and transparency.

Finally, pharmacovigilance planning should incorporate mechanisms for continuous improvement, such as regular review and evaluation of safety data, and the implementation of corrective actions as needed. This helps to ensure that the pharmacovigilance system remains effective and responsive to emerging safety issues.

18.7 Good clinical practice in pharmacovigilance studies

Good Clinical Practice (GCP) guidelines provide a framework for the design, conduct, and reporting of clinical trials to ensure that the rights, safety, and well-being of human subjects are protected and that the data collected from these trials are reliable and robust. In the context of pharmacovigilance, GCP guidelines provide a set of ethical and scientific standards that should be followed when conducting studies aimed at assessing the safety of drugs and other medical products.

GCP guidelines cover a wide range of topics, including the responsibilities of investigators, sponsors, and regulatory authorities; the selection and recruitment of study participants; the design of clinical trials; the monitoring and reporting of adverse events; and the handling and analysis of study data. Some of the key principles of GCP that are particularly relevant to pharmacovigilance studies include:

Informed Consent: GCP guidelines emphasize the importance of obtaining informed consent from study participants before they are enrolled in a clinical trial. In the context of pharmacovigilance, this means that individuals should be informed about the potential risks and benefits of participating in a study aimed at assessing the safety of a drug or other medical product, and they should be given the opportunity to ask questions and to withdraw from the study at any time.

Ethics: GCP guidelines require that clinical trials be conducted in an ethical manner, with due consideration for the welfare of the study participants. In the context of pharmacovigilance studies, this means that measures should be taken to minimize the risks associated with participation, and that any adverse events that occur should be reported promptly and accurately.

Data Integrity: GCP guidelines require that the data collected in clinical trials be accurate, complete, and verifiable. In the context of pharmacovigilance studies, this means that measures should be taken to ensure that adverse events are recorded in a standardized and consistent manner, and that the data collected are analyzed and reported in a transparent and objective manner.

Monitoring: GCP guidelines require that clinical trials be monitored to ensure that they are being conducted in compliance with the protocol and with applicable regulations and guidelines.

In the context of pharmacovigilance studies, this means that the safety of study participants should be monitored closely, and that any adverse events that occur should be reported and investigated promptly.

Reporting: GCP guidelines require that the results of clinical trials be reported accurately and in a timely manner. In the context of pharmacovigilance studies, this means that any adverse events that occur should be reported promptly to the appropriate regulatory authorities, and that the results of the study should be disseminated in a transparent and objective manner.

XIX

Pharmacogenomics of adverse reactions

19.1 Pharmacogenomics of adverse drug reactions

Pharmacogenomics is the study of genetic variations that influence an individual's response to drugs. Adverse drug reactions (ADRs) are unwanted or harmful reactions to medications that can range from mild to severe. Pharmacogenomics has emerged as a promising approach to identify genetic factors that contribute to ADRs.

The field of pharmacogenomics is rapidly growing, and there is a significant interest in its application in pharmacovigilance. Pharmacovigilance is the process of monitoring and evaluating adverse drug reactions to ensure safe and effective use of medications. By understanding the genetic factors that contribute to ADRs, pharmacovigilance can be improved to identify patients who are at risk of ADRs and to develop personalized treatments based on their genetic makeup.

Pharmacogenetics is an important area of pharmacovigilance that focuses on identifying how genetic variations can influence an individual's response to medication. The genetic variations can affect various pharmacokinetic (PK) parameters such as drug metabolism, absorption, distribution, and elimination.

For example, individuals who carry a genetic variation in the CYP2D6 gene may have reduced drug metabolism capacity and are at a higher risk of developing adverse drug reactions (ADRs) when taking drugs that are metabolized by this enzyme. This can lead to increased drug levels in the blood, which may result in toxicity.CYP2D6 gene is involved in the metabolism of several drugs, including codeine and tamoxifen. Patients who have certain variants of this gene may have an increased risk of experiencing ADRs when taking these medications.

Another example is the genetic variation in the TPMT gene, which can affect the metabolism of the immunosuppressant drug, azathioprine. Patients who carry a genetic variant associated with reduced TPMT activity may experience severe bone marrow suppression and other toxicities when taking the drug at standard doses.

In addition to PK parameters, genetic variations can also influence pharmacodynamic (PD) parameters, such as drug target expression, binding affinity, and downstream signaling. For example, a genetic variant in the HLA gene has been associated with an increased risk of developing a severe skin reaction called Stevens-Johnson syndrome/toxic epidermal necrolysis (SJS/TEN) in patients treated with the anticonvulsant drug, carbamazepine. The variant alters the HLA protein structure, leading to an immune response that causes skin cell death.

Pharmacogenomics can also be used to develop biomarkers that can predict which patients are at risk of ADRs. For example, genetic variants in the UGT1A1 gene have been associated with an increased risk of toxicity to the chemotherapy drug irinotecan. Testing for these variants can help identify patients who are at risk of toxicity and adjust the dosage of the medication accordingly.

Pharmacogenomics has emerged as a promising approach to improve pharmacovigilance and prevent ADRs. By identifying genetic factors that contribute to ADRs, personalized treatments can be developed to ensure safe and effective use of medications.

19.1 Drug safety evaluation in special populations:

Drug safety evaluation in special populations such as pediatrics, pregnancy and lactation, and geriatrics is crucial to ensure safe and effective use of medications. These populations are particularly vulnerable to adverse drug reactions (ADRs) due to physiological and pharmacological differences.

19.1.1 Pediatrics

Introduction: Pediatrics refers to the medical care of infants, children, and adolescents. The safety and efficacy of drugs in this population is of great importance due to their unique characteristics and the potential long-term consequences of drug exposure. Pharmacovigilance is essential in ensuring the safety of drugs used in pediatrics, as adverse drug reactions (ADRs) can have severe consequences in this population.

Pharmacokinetic Differences in Pediatrics: Pharmacokinetics refers to the study of the movement of drugs within the body, including absorption, distribution, metabolism, and elimination. In pediatrics, there are significant differences in pharmacokinetics compared to adults. These differences are due to the rapid changes in growth and development in children, which can lead to variability in drug exposure and response.

For example, infants have a higher percentage of body water and lower body fat than adults, which can affect drug distribution. Additionally, the activity of drug-metabolizing enzymes and renal function are immature in neonates, which can result in altered drug clearance. The importance of age, weight, and body surface area in pediatric pharmacokinetics cannot be overstated, as dosing adjustments are often required to ensure appropriate drug exposure.

Adverse Drug Reactions in Pediatrics: ADRs are a significant concern in pediatrics, as children may be more susceptible to adverse events due to their smaller size and immature organ function. Common ADRs in children include gastrointestinal disturbances, dermatological reactions, and neuropsychiatric events. Special considerations must be taken for ADRs in neonates, infants, and older children. For example, neonates may be at risk for kernicterus, a severe form of brain damage caused by the buildup of bilirubin, which can result from the use of certain medications.

Challenges in Clinical Trials for Pediatrics: Ethical considerations in conducting clinical trials in children are paramount, as children cannot provide informed consent. The use of placebo controls in clinical trials may be ethically questionable, as children may be placed at risk without receiving any potential benefit from the experimental treatment. Additionally, determining appropriate dosages, safety, and efficacy in pediatric populations can be challenging due to the variability in pharmacokinetics and the limited available data.

Regulatory Considerations for Pediatric Drug Safety Evaluation: The Pediatric Research Equity Act (PREA) and the Best Pharmaceuticals for Children Act (BPCA) were enacted in the United States to promote pediatric drug development and safety. PREA requires pharmaceutical companies to conduct pediatric studies for drugs intended for use in children, while BPCA provides financial incentives for companies to conduct pediatric studies for off-patent drugs. The US Food and Drug Administration (FDA) plays a critical role in pediatric drug safety evaluation and approval, providing guidance to companies regarding the design of pediatric clinical trials and the assessment of safety and efficacy in this population.

Current Research in Pediatric Pharmacovigilance: Advances in technology and pharmacogenomics have improved our understanding of pediatric drug safety. Pharmacogenomics refers to the study of how genetic variations can affect drug response. For example, a genetic variant in the enzyme responsible for metabolizing codeine to its active form can result in life-threatening respiratory depression in children. Patient registries and post-marketing surveillance can also be valuable tools for monitoring pediatric drug safety, allowing for the identification of potential

ADRs that may not have been detected in clinical trials.

Case Study: A recent example of the importance of pediatric pharmacovigilance is the safety of acetaminophen in infants. Acetaminophen is commonly used to treat pain and fever in infants and young children. However, studies have shown that excessive use or overdosing of acetaminophen can cause liver damage. This highlights the need for careful dosing and monitoring in this population. Additionally, a recent study found that certain genetic variants can affect the metabolism of acetaminophen in children, leading to potential toxicity. Pharmacogenomic testing can help identify these individuals and guide dosing recommendations. This case study illustrates the importance of considering both pharmacokinetic and genetic factors in pediatric drug safety evaluation. It also emphasizes the need for ongoing monitoring and research to ensure the safe use of medications in this vulnerable population.

19.1.2 Pregnancy and Lactation:

Pregnancy and lactation are unique physiological states that can impact drug safety evaluation. Pregnancy involves complex changes in maternal physiology and fetal development, while lactation involves the production and secretion of breast milk. The safety of medications used during pregnancy and lactation is a critical concern for healthcare providers and patients. The field of pharmacovigilance plays a crucial role in monitoring drug safety in these populations.

1. Pharmacokinetic differences in pregnancy and lactation

Pregnancy and lactation can affect the absorption, distribution, metabolism, and elimination of drugs in the body. Changes in maternal physiology, such as alterations in gastric pH and increased blood volume, can impact drug absorption. Changes in maternal body composition and distribution of body fluids can also affect drug distribution. Metabolism and elimination of drugs can be altered due to changes in maternal hepatic and renal function. Understanding these differences is critical in evaluating drug safety during pregnancy and lactation.

2. Adverse drug reactions in pregnancy and lactation

Pregnant and lactating women are at risk of experiencing adverse drug reactions. Common adverse reactions in these populations include nausea, vomiting, and headaches. However, special considerations must be given to the potential effects on the developing fetus and the breastfed infant. Certain medications, such as ACE inhibitors, can cause fetal renal failure when used during pregnancy, while others, such as antidepressants, can cause neonatal withdrawal symptoms when used during lactation.

3. Challenges in clinical trials for pregnancy and lactation

Conducting clinical trials in pregnant and lactating women presents ethical challenges. Pregnant women are often excluded from clinical trials due to concerns about fetal safety, leaving a significant gap in knowledge about the safety and efficacy of medications in this population. The use of animal models and extrapolation from non-pregnant populations may be necessary to fill this gap. Additionally, determining appropriate dosages can be challenging, as maternal physiology can affect drug metabolism and elimination.

4. Regulatory considerations for pregnancy and lactation

drug safety evaluation The FDA and other regulatory agencies play a critical role in evaluating the safety of medications used during pregnancy and lactation. The Pregnancy and Lactation Labeling Rule (PLLR) was introduced in 2015 to provide more comprehensive information about the safety of medications during pregnancy and lactation. The rule requires labeling information to include information about the potential risks to the developing fetus and breastfed infants.

5. Current research in pregnancy and lactation

pharmacovigilance Advances in technology and pharmacogenomics have led to new approaches to evaluating drug safety during pregnancy and lactation. Patient registries and post-marketing surveillance can provide valuable data on the safety of medications in these populations. The use of pharmacogenomic testing can help identify genetic factors that may affect drug metabolism and elimination in pregnant and lactating women.

Case Study: The tragedy of thalidomide serves as a stark reminder of the importance of pharmacovigilance in pregnancy. Thalidomide, a drug marketed in the 1950s and 1960s as a treatment for morning sickness, was later found to cause severe birth defects, such as limb abnormalities and phocomelia. The devastating consequences of thalidomide use led to increased scrutiny of drug safety in pregnancy and the development of the Pregnancy and Lactation Labeling Rule. This case highlights the need for ongoing monitoring and evaluation of drug safety in pregnant and lactating women.

19.1.3 Geriatrics:

Geriatrics is a branch of medicine that focuses on the health and care of elderly individuals. Geriatric pharmacology refers to the study of drug use in the elderly population, taking into account the unique physiological changes that occur with aging. The aging process can cause changes in pharmacokinetics and pharmacodynamics, which can increase the risk of adverse drug reactions (ADRs) in the elderly. This makes drug safety evaluation in geriatric populations a critical concern.

1.Pharmacokinetic differences in geriatrics

There are several pharmacokinetic differences that occur with aging, including changes in drug absorption, distribution, metabolism, and elimination. Age-related changes in body composition, such as decreased muscle mass and increased body fat, can alter drug distribution. Additionally, changes in renal and hepatic function can affect drug metabolism and elimination. Elderly individuals are also more likely to have comorbidities and take multiple medications, which can result in drug-drug interactions and impact pharmacokinetics.

2.Adverse drug reactions in geriatrics

Elderly individuals are at an increased risk of experiencing ADRs due to changes in pharmacokinetics and the presence of comorbidities. Common ADRs in geriatrics include falls, delirium, gastrointestinal bleeding, and renal impairment. There are also certain medications that are known to cause ADRs in elderly individuals, such as benzodiazepines and anticholinergics.

3. Challenges in clinical trials for geriatrics

Conducting clinical trials in elderly individuals can be challenging due to ethical considerations and difficulties in recruitment. Elderly individuals may have multiple comorbidities and take multiple medications, which can complicate the determination of appropriate dosage, safety, and efficacy of investigational drugs. Additionally, elderly individuals may be less likely to participate in clinical trials due to concerns about potential risks.

4. Regulatory considerations for geriatric drug safety evaluation

The FDA and other regulatory agencies have specific guidelines for drug safety evaluation in geriatric populations. The Geriatric Research, Education, and Clinical Center (GRECC) was established by the Department of Veterans Affairs to improve the care of elderly veterans and promote research in geriatrics.

5. Current research in geriatric pharmacovigilance

Advances in technology and pharmacogenomics are being utilized to improve drug safety evaluation in geriatric populations. Patient registries and post-marketing surveillance are also important tools for monitoring ADRs in elderly individuals.

Case Study: A recent example of the importance of pharmacovigilance in geriatrics is the safety of antipsychotic medications in elderly individuals with dementia. Antipsychotics are commonly used to treat behavioral symptoms in individuals with dementia, but have been associated with an increased risk of death. The FDA issued a black box warning for antipsychotics in elderly individuals with dementia in 2005, highlighting the importance of rigorous drug safety evaluation in this population. A study published in JAMA Psychiatry in 2018 found that the use of antipsychotics in elderly individuals with dementia was associated with a higher risk of mortality compared to non-use. This study underscores the importance of ongoing drug safety evaluation in geriatric populations to ensure the safe use of medications.

XX

Miscellaneous

20.1 CIOMS

CIOMS (**Council for International Organizations of Medical Sciences**) is a non-governmental organization that was founded in 1949 to promote research and education in the field of medical sciences. Over the years, CIOMS has become a leading international organization that collaborates with the World Health Organization (WHO) and other international organizations to develop ethical guidelines for medical research, pharmacovigilance, and drug safety evaluation.

One of the key activities of CIOMS is the formation of working groups that bring together experts from various disciplines to address important issues related to medical research and drug safety. These working groups develop guidelines and recommendations based on the latest scientific evidence and ethical principles. Some examples of CIOMS working groups include the Pharmacovigilance Working Group, the Ethical Issues in Medical Research Working Group, and the Genetically Modified Organisms in Research Working Group.

The CIOMS Form is one of the most widely used guidelines developed by CIOMS. The form is a standardized tool for reporting adverse drug reactions and includes detailed information about the patient, the drug, and the adverse event. Healthcare professionals and drug regulatory agencies around the world use the CIOMS Form to report and monitor adverse drug reactions. The form helps to ensure that adverse drug reactions are reported in a consistent and standardized manner, which is important for identifying potential safety issues associated with a particular drug.

Moreover, the CIOMS Form is designed to collect critical information that can be used to assess the causal relationship between the drug and the adverse event, as well as the severity and outcome of the event. This information is essential for identifying and understanding the risks associated with the use of a drug, and for making informed decisions about its safety and efficacy.

The CIOMS Form is also a valuable tool for post-marketing surveillance of drugs. It enables healthcare professionals and regulatory agencies to monitor the safety of drugs after they have been approved for use, and to identify and respond to any emerging safety concerns. By collecting and analyzing data on adverse drug reactions, regulatory agencies can make informed decisions about the need for additional safety measures, such as changes to the labeling or restrictions on the use of a drug.

In addition to the CIOMS Form, CIOMS has also developed guidelines for ethical considerations in medical research involving human subjects, the use of genetically modified organisms in research, and the use of biobanks for medical research. These guidelines are widely used by researchers, healthcare professionals, and regulatory agencies around the world. The ethical guidelines for medical research provide a framework for conducting research in a responsible and ethical manner while ensuring that the rights and welfare of human subjects are protected. The guidelines for genetically modified organisms in research provide guidance on the ethical considerations related to the use of genetically modified organisms in research. The guidelines for biobanks provide guidance on the ethical considerations related to the collection, storage, and use of biological samples for medical research.

Furthermore, CIOMS collaborates with other international organizations, such as the WHO and the International Council for Harmonization of Technical Requirements for Pharmaceuticals for Human Use (ICH), to develop harmonized guidelines and recommendations for medical research and drug safety evaluation. This collaboration helps to ensure that guidelines and recommendations are consistent across different countries and regions, which is important for ensuring patient safety and for facilitating global drug development.

20.2 CIOMS working Groups:

CIOMS Working Groups are collaborative groups of experts from different disciplines and geographic regions who come together to develop guidelines and recommendations on important issues related to medical research and drug safety. These working groups are composed of experts in fields such as clinical medicine, pharmacology, epidemiology, and bioethics.

CIOMS working groups are created to address specific topics or issues in the field of medical research and drug safety. The groups use a collaborative approach to review the available evidence, identify knowledge gaps, and develop evidence-based recommendations that reflect the latest scientific and ethical principles.

Some examples of CIOMS working groups include the Working Group on Vaccine Pharmacovigilance, the Working Group on Drug-induced Liver Injury, and the Working Group on Drug Interactions. Each of these groups is focused on a specific topic, and their work helps to improve the safety and effectiveness of vaccines, drugs, and other medical treatments.

The members of CIOMS working groups come from a variety of organizations, including government agencies, academic institutions, and non-governmental organizations. The groups typically work over a period of several years to develop their recommendations, and the final products are widely disseminated and used by healthcare professionals, researchers, and drug regulatory agencies around the world.

20.3 The Drugs and Cosmetics Act (D&C Act) and Schedule Y

The Drugs and Cosmetics Act (D&C Act) and Schedule Y are two important pieces of legislation in India that govern the regulation of drugs and clinical trials. The D&C Act, 1940, and Rules, 1945, provide the legal framework for the import, manufacture, distribution, and sale of drugs in India. Schedule Y outlines the requirements and guidelines for conducting clinical trials in India. These regulations require pharmaceutical companies to conduct clinical trials in accordance with good clinical practice (GCP) guidelines and to follow strict ethical standards.

CDSCO:

The Central Drugs Standard Control Organization (CDSCO) is the national regulatory body of India that is responsible for the regulation of pharmaceuticals and medical devices. CDSCO is an important stakeholder in pharmacovigilance, which is the science and activities relating to the detection, assessment, understanding, and prevention of adverse effects or any other drug-related problems.

In recent years, CDSCO has made significant efforts to improve pharmacovigilance in India. The Pharmacovigilance Program of India (PvPI) was launched in 2010 as a collaborative initiative between CDSCO and the Indian Pharmacopoeia Commission (IPC) to monitor the safety of drugs in India. PvPI aims to collect, collate, and analyze adverse drug reactions (ADRs) reported by healthcare professionals and consumers in India. The program also provides training and education to healthcare professionals and consumers on pharmacovigilance.

20.4 Differences in Indian and global pharmacovigilance requirements

One of the key differences between Indian and global pharmacovigilance requirements is the scope of the pharmacovigilance program. While the pharmacovigilance programs in many developed countries focus on monitoring ADRs for drugs that have already been approved and are on the market, the Indian pharmacovigilance program also includes the monitoring of ADRs during clinical trials. This is because India is a major hub for clinical trials, and the CDSCO has recognized the need for robust pharmacovigilance during the clinical trial phase as well.

Another difference is the reporting requirements for ADRs. In India, healthcare professionals and pharmaceutical companies are required to report serious ADRs within 15 days, while non-serious ADRs should be reported within 90 days. In many other countries, the reporting requirements for ADRs are less strict and may vary depending on the severity of the reaction and other factors.

Furthermore, India has a unique system for monitoring ADRs called the Indian Pharmacopoeia Commission (IPC). The IPC is responsible for monitoring and reporting ADRs, and it has established a national center for pharmacovigilance in collaboration with the CDSCO. The IPC also maintains a national database of ADRs, which is used by healthcare professionals and regulatory authorities to monitor drug safety.